*"If the only way to heal painful high school memories is to laugh at someone else's painful high school memories, this book can accurately be labeled the antidote. . . . Illustrated with great awkward-phase photos, this treasure-chest of confusion and angst will make readers squirm and smile with the realization that, as Nadelberg put it, 'we were all that same strange kid.'"
—*Publishers Weekly* (Starred Review)

"Heartbreakingly hilarious tales of personal woe and social catastrophe." —*Flavorpill*

"Indulge in this collection of cringe-worthy (and often hilarious) stories framed with insight from their now grown-up writers." —*OK!*

"The most woeful tales of teenage anguish." —*Reuters*

"Spreading the new gospel of awkward all over the land."
—*DailyCandy*

"It makes readers laugh and . . . reminisce about their own fumbling attempts at expressing hormone-fueled emotions."
—*Chicago Tribune*

"You won't be able to put this one down." —*ELLEgirl*

"Embarrassing, hilarious, and just plain wrong."
—*BUST* magazine

"*Mortified* is ungainly innocent and awkwardly charming with a bite of reality." —*Entertainment Today*

Love Is a Battlefield

M♥RTIFIED

Love Is a Battlefield

COLLECTED BY
DAVID NADELBERG

Contributing Editors:
Shay DeGrandis
Annette Ferrara
Anne Jensen
Neil Katcher
Scott Lifton
Jenny Ruth Myers
Giulia Rozzi
Brandy Barber
Heather Van Atta

SIMON SPOTLIGHT ENTERTAINMENT
New York   London   Toronto   Sydney

S|S|E

SIMON SPOTLIGHT ENTERTAINMENT

An imprint of Simon & Schuster, Inc.

1230 Avenue of the Americas, New York, New York 10020

SIMON SPOTLIGHT ENTERTAINMENT and related logo are trademarks of
Simon & Schuster, Inc.

Designed by Yaffa Jaskoll

Manufactured in the United States of America

First Edition 10 9 8 7 6 5 4 3 2 1

Library of Congress Cataloging-in-Publication Data

Mortified : love is a battlefield / collected by David Nadelberg. — 1st ed.

p. cm.

ISBN-13: 978-1-4169-5479-8 (pbk.)

ISBN-10: 1-4169-5479-1 (pbk.)

1. Teenagers' writings, American. 2. American wit and humor. 3.
Adolescence—Literary collections. 4. Anxiety—Literary collections.

I. Nadelberg, David.

PS508.T44M666 2008

810.8'09283--dc22

2007033690

**MORTIFIED is about our
relationships to memory.**

**This book is for Judy, who continues to offer a
lifetime of great memories.**

Love's the word. Only one
of the day ♡ ♡ ♡ ♡

—*Charles Young, Journal, Age 16*

to all of those
who have
hurt.

—*Shay DeGrandis, Poetry Notebook, Age 18*

THANGST!

We're thrilled to have the following BFFs in our lives to offer the support that helped make our second book possible: Ben Acker, Sarah Faith Alterman, Anne Altman, Curtis Armstrong, Bill Barminski, Marty Barrett, Leah Bathe, Ben Blacker, Judy Blume, Jessica Bogli, Bill Byrne, Lia Buman, Meg Cabot, Cheryl Calegari, Hillary Carlip, Karen Corday, Egan and Susan Danehy, James Denton, Andi Gabrick, Eddie Gamarra, Annie Girard, Green Mill Lounge, Anastasia Goodstein, Kirsten Gronfield, Abby Gross, Annabelle Gurwitch, Angel and Kevin Herlihy, Perrin Iacopino, Dmitri Johnson, Sydell Katcher, King King, Thomas King, Krista Lanphear, Erica Lies, Kiki L'Italien, Makor, Make-Out Room, Frank Matthews, Erika May, Mo Pitkin's House of Satisfaction, Sarah Grace McCandless, Kevin McDonald, Matt McDonald, Marc McTizic, Bruce Miller, Stephen and Judy Nadelberg, Tim Owens, the Paradise Lounge, Shaun Parker, Elena and John Pellegrino, Mark Phinney, Ed, Pingol, Busy Philipps, Sascha Rothchild, Jami Rudofsky, Eddie Schmidt, Adam Schwitters, Will Seymour, Simon Spotlight Entertainment, Law Tarello, Kevin Tidwell, the staff at *This American Life* (Ira, Jane, Julie, Jorge, and more), Christian Wolf, Elijah Wood, Anne Woodward, Megan Zabel, Gwynne Zink, Jason Zwolinski, the Mortified After School Orchestra (Renee Albert, Gordon Bash, Mark Beltzman, Andrew Glazier, Ethel Lung, Adam Smith, and more), all our fans everywhere.

Finally . . . thanks to our fearless editor, Patrick Price, for agreeing to throw all time-honored rules of grammar out the door.

INTRODUCTION

As adults, we're fascinated by the subject of love and lust. Ballads dominate pop radio. Sex scandals stalk CNN. Dating sites boast more subscribers than most magazines.

As kids, our curiosity about romance is even more intense. After all, we don't just like someone. We *like* like someone. We don't just flirt. We fixate.

The voices captured in the pages that follow are like brave little explorers surveying foreign soil, desperately hoping to make sense of the terrain. Some are cautious. Some are reckless. All are clueless. Imagine Lewis and Clark lost in the pages of a Judy Blume novel.

We spend our whole lives trying to understand that terrain. Hell, even asexual people—from monks to Morrissey—struggle to make sense of it. And regardless of whether we are pining for it, experiencing it, or alienated from it, each of us manages to emerge from the ashes of adolescence with our own personal interpretation.

From the first kiss to the first rejection to all the thrills that fall in between, the following entries chronicle our early awkward attempts to understand the one word that we never quite master anyway: love.

Through delusional displays of celebrity obsession, prudish outbursts of hand-holding, and disturbing sexual awakenings, *whatever* we discover about romance during our adolescent expeditions is what we carry with us for the rest of our lives.

As such, we hope you'll see this collection as we do: an overdue Valentine to those confused kids we left behind on the bright yellow bus.

After all, they deserve some action.

A NOTE TO THE READER

To protect the innocent, awkward, and angsty, some of the names, dates, places, and other identifying details in this book have been altered.

Sadly, everything else is true.

As is the nature of *Mortified*'s commitment to authenticity, no language has ever been added to the source material or rewritten for the sake of entertainment. Material is selected and then presented around unique narrative themes that emerge from the author's life.

In short, these kids really wrote this crap.

TABLE OF CONTENTS

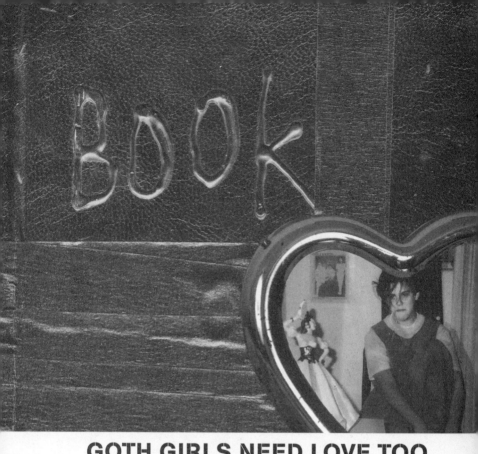

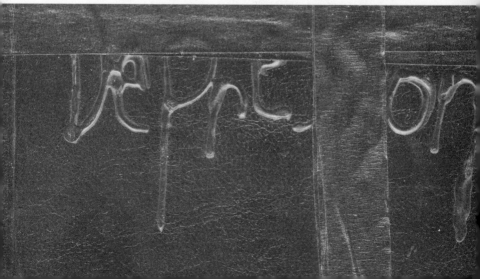

GOTH GIRLS NEED LOVE TOO

Shay DeGrandis

Most Likely to . . . Be Institutionalized

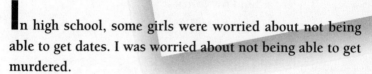

In high school, some girls were worried about not being able to get dates. I was worried about not being able to get murdered.

I had convinced myself that I was completely unlovable. I attempted to have the upper hand, however, by purposefully making myself *appear* undesirable so I wouldn't have to worry about actually *being* undesirable.

I presented myself as a miserable wreck of a girl— tangled disarray of black hair, paler than a ghost, always walking around looking sullen and angry. Outside, I looked like a depressed mess. Inside, however, I was really just one big raging hormone. I often fantasized that Robert Smith, the lead singer of the Cure, was totally in love with me. Obviously, he couldn't *really* be in love with me on account of the fact that I was unlovable.

So in my lonely yearning I wrote many poems in my journal—a black book on which I scrawled "Book of Depression" in black puffy paint. These helped me get out my teenage sexual frustration and were a way to let Mr. Smith know how exactly I felt about him.

Untitled

So you say you have
    always wanted to commit

3

a murder and get
away with it?
Kill me. PLEASE.
Wrap your long, white,
wedding-banded
fingers around my throat,
look into my eyes with
your small, brown irises
until mine drop into blackness
and my sight
and breath are gone
forever.
kiss my purple-tinted lips
with your red-stained ones
until mine are stained with
your loss.
no one could ever murder me
as well as you,
my god.
And no one ever will.

Untitled

The flat character
looks up at him
The sad, unsatisfied god.
She is worried, so she prays.
It is no help.
He is too sad to grant wishes
or answer prayers.

She wishes she could do something
    but it is no use
He is in a world too far away
        for her to see or smell.

Untitled

Speeding along in my compact space of metal, glass
and rubber
I feel like God—able to do what I please to anyone I
please.
Synonymous to the red blood cell on the rural
Artery on the way home.
I can see far ahead of me on the highway
As I realize that there is another vehicle
Coming from the other direction.
I recognize the driver—my love for him immense.
I race faster towards him, my heart beating
And increasing with the speed of the car.
I can feel warmth like no other as I envision
My vehicle moving into his lane and
Realize that I have already done so without
Enough time to turn back.
                    Blackness.
I open my eyes to see that the artery has
Burst, across my windshield the blood is
Spattered in a mixture of flesh and glass.
The idol lay dead, his face inches from mine
Which is stuck on-to the steering wheel.
But he is not dead yet, he moves,

Enough for me to look into his eyes
And ask him if it was as good
For him as it was for me. I stop,
Knowing that the line was too commonplace for
The God on my windshield. so I closed my eyes and
shuffled off this mortal coil.

THE BIBLICAL SENSE

Leslie McLean

Most Likely to . . . Lose Her Virginity

The beauty
of God's love
fills all my days
with joy!

Leslie S. McLean

In high school I vacillated between being extremely horny and a very active member of the Ukiah First Presbyterian Church youth group and Bible study. As such, I was a militant virgin and a compulsive masturbator.

Over the course of six months I set out to find God, only to discover something else as well.

12-14-87

Sexual frustration. I constantly dwell on this subject. Perhaps God put trials on earth for people and mine is good-looking beautiful males. It is the thorn in my side–that which prevents me from furthering my spiritual growth. I need to be gently touched, physically, emotionally, spiritually. I touch others, but Jesus is the only one who touches me.

1-13-88

I was reading a book about major religions and I found the basic truths of Buddhism to have significance.
1. All life is suffering. (ie sexual frustration)
2. Suffering is caused by craving (ie wanting, lusting and not satisfying desires)

9

3. Deny earthly cravings.
4. Transcend—become Buddha, enlightened one.

A Christian can transcend as well. Perhaps I need more meditation, more dedication to other people, more time in prayer, Bible study. No, not perhaps, I do need to do this. I must be a rebel, as was Christ!

1-21-88
The drive to Tahoe is so boring. Wendy is so infatuated with this guy and she can't stop talking about him. We get there and Jeff, Greg, Brady and I build a snow sculpture of a penis complete with a garden hose. It was a riot. Then we steal some rum from a cabin. Brady is sexy. After Bible study we all goof around until Wendy gives me a lecture about how out of line my behavior is. True I was obnoxious, but it really bugs me when everyone is too prudish to enjoy themselves.

1-29-88
I have three earrings in my right ear. I did this myself last night but this morning is not beautiful. I am happy with myself until I think about my life. I fantasize about marvelous men who are non existent in my life so I masturbate (I hate that word) for sexual fulfillment but my state of frustration continues. I have so much desire, creativity, imagination, sensuality, sensitivity but with whom may I share these feelings?

2-14-88

Sometimes I wish I were a guy. Guys are kinder than women. Women are highly sensitive and creative individuals thus causing them to be raging bitches. Women are manipulative, cunning, back-stabbing gossiping snags. Guys are oblivious, susceptible, sexually active, misguided lost people, but they are sweet. I would be a wonderful guy—so sexy. My body, hair style, looks would be uniquely exquisite. I would be a swimmer, a rad guitar player and an accomplished actor. Tons of girls would lust after me—I would see most of them as utterly foolish, but there would be some friends, females, who would keenly see my value as a human being.

2-29-88

I started out ugly in junior high. Awkward, boyish, big nose, no make up, no breasts, nerdy clothes. Then like a flower I bloomed into a young woman. I keep getting more beautiful on the inside and out and my father says I will continue to do so. I think my body developed in a perfect sequence. I have a beautiful body—shapely legs, curvy slim hips, large full breasts, interesting face structure, blue/green eyes, shiny golden hair, perfect teeth, a big smile and a tall 5'8" body. I need to lose 15 pounds to attain bodily perfection though . . . Right now I am a blob, but come summer I will be gorgeous!!

3-10-88

I will be 18 soon, a legal adult punishable by law in the adult courts. So before I reach this turning point . . . I must rape the little ones. Perhaps I will briefly indulge in Todd, a sophomore to be completed by a triumphant act with the unbearably gorgeous freshman Brian. It is so sad that these two are underclassmen. Being a senior girl is difficult. There are no desirable men in my class and I have gotten to the point of self-assurance that I don't care what others think of what I do.

I must rape the little ones.

4-11-88

Yesterday I went to Chris's house. Chris is my current mate. I went over and brought my guitar and stood there and played for Chris and his very fuckable little gorgeous freshman brother Brian. I played my version of the Cure's "Boys Don't Cry." I really embarrassed myself which is terrible. The problem is Chris is too hung up on coolness to get into my eccentricities.

Maybe I should shave my legs, dress wonderfully, stop playing my guitar along with my stereo with no lights on while wearing my underwear. I shouldn't laugh out loud, I shouldn't dance like a freak. I should calm down. I shouldn't sleep in the nude, model for my mirrors, dance with only my garter belt on. I shouldn't press my breasts against the icy glass to see my nipples get hard. I shouldn't swim seductively, skinny dipping when I get the chance. I shouldn't dance with my flowing pareau and stay up reading and writing. I am self confident and happy and therefore a threat to the existence of insecure people.

4-30-88
Yesterday I took an adventurous walk in the rain through the hills and valleys behind my house. I crossed creeks, hopped fences and got lost. I finally came to my secret grove as the sun began to set. I took off my shirt and bra and laid down breasts first in the wet grass. I thought about Dustin Welch and the Indians of Ancient Days and I came. I am a very sexual person!

6-10-88
Jay keeps finger banging me in the hot tub. We'll be there with many people talking, then we start teasing each other with our hands and feet. Before too long, he is touching me in the forbidden THERE and I indulge while other people in the tub continue chatting in celibacy. I smile and talk like nothing is happening but something is definitely happening. I just get such a charge from attractive people. How superficial I am with relationships!

Well a certainly sexually frustrating day. I must be near menstruation. But today was Bible study. How wonderful it is to sing praises to God. I feel my spirit singing inside of me reaching and connecting with God. It makes me elated with euphoric tears in my eyes.

I have such a different view of religion. I'm happy or mad with God, not usually sad and overly emotional. Joy or anger. God I want sunshine. I want to be beautiful. I feel beautiful. I am beautiful. If only I could stop my chocolate addiction. I need help, I shake, my eyes water. I satisfy my sexual needs with chocolate. Maybe I should stick a chocolate bar inside my warm moist vagina. It would melt. Then I would die.

Did you know I can fold my tongue? Yes I can. Then I flick it out like a lizard. I am a reptile. Then why do I have allergies? Wow, I can't wait to graduate. I run naked with anticipation. School is a sweet slow hell. Wouldn't it be wonderful to be a fish? To live underwater with your entire body engulfed in aquamarine joy. Water is so beautiful. I hate wearing a swimsuit. I am a liberated woman . . . FREE! Oh I smile a knowing smile. I am detached from everyone. I look older, much older than everyone here at school. I am older and more independent.

End of Summer 1988

Jay came into my life on June 10, 1988. He had long flowing blonde hair, a lean tone body, a keen interest in nature, a confidence and aura which molded and entwined with my spirit. We were so in synch, on the same wave. Beautiful, glowing—yet self-indulgent drinking wine and smoking cloves. Jay made other relationships and boys seem obsolete. Jay was all. I was so attracted to him.

We made love in Berkeley at the Marriot Marina on July 20, 1988. We were too in tune with each other—out of touch with God. Yet we did make love again and again. Uniting our bodies, souls and minds in a way which is less than the best. More wrong than right. Yet so incredible, so powerful and moving.

ADULT ME SAYS:

And that is how I finally lost my virginity to a visiting Mormon delinquint from Utah. It turns out that Jay is currently employed at a Vegas hotel. As for me, I am still a horny Presbyterian.

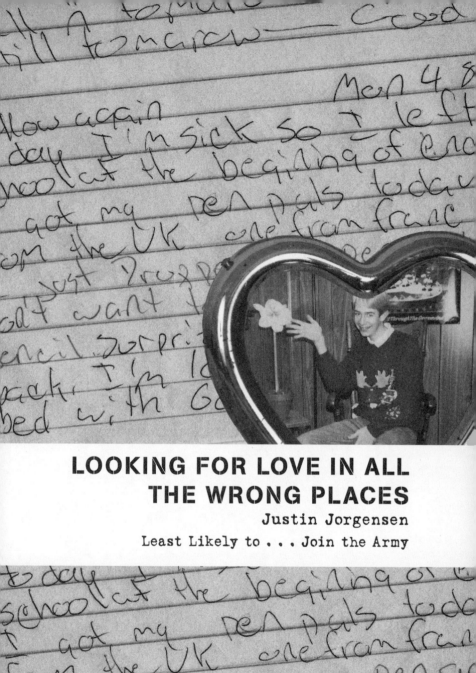

LOOKING FOR LOVE IN ALL THE WRONG PLACES

Justin Jorgensen

Least Likely to . . . Join the Army

In seventh grade I realized I was gay. And although this was in Fargo, North Dakota, I did manage to find a couple of gay friends. But those friendships were born from circumstance and maintained by necessity, not desire.

Through my remaining high school years, I continued to search for a more fulfilling relationship with someone I actually wanted to be with. These journal entries were typed on my Amiga 3000 beginning in 1988, when I was thirteen, and span the following six years.

Jon is a jerk! Uncle Gene thinks I'm a fag because I like stickers. That's ok, he's a jerk too. Tom Montague died his hair auburn and wants me to call him Bernie. My mom says Sam and Tom are a bad influence on me. She thinks they're turning me into a fag. I don't see how they could be a bad influence. Tom is on the honor roll.

I just thought I'd list the good and bad things about Sam.
Bad:
He's not like me
My parents dislike him
He thinks negative
Acts stupid

Weird
Fat
Boring
Unattractive
Never compliments me
People think we're gay

Good:
He's my age
He's in my grade

Sam jacked me off tonight while we watched my
video.

ADULT ME SAYS:

The "video" was actually a tape I'd shot of myself masturbating.

He wants me to make one for Steve.

Sam doesn't like me jacking him off. I sucked his
a couple of times . . . but sex is so boring really. Liz
is bisexual. However I don't really give a shit. I love
popping zits.

After eating at Randy's a couple days ago, Mom
said, "Sooooo . . . would you consider yourself . . .
homosexual . . . heterosexual?"

"I like to think of myself as sexually open-minded,"
I said. A complete lie. Granted, I do believe there are
true bisexuals, but I'm not one of them.

There was the most beautiful creature at Frank's Nursery today, looked just like Jason Priestley only so much better and so much more likeable. We exchanged several glances. But I'm not sure he's gay. Why couldn't all gay people be born green or something, so we'd know. I heard this noise and I found him standing there all over this spilled fertilizer on the floor.

There was a gay dance at a local hotel on Saturday. I wore my strut-n-slut outfit consisting of brown leather boots, well-worn blue jeans with almost a hole in the knee, long-sleeve white tee with my leather vest, and light tan sports coat. I know I looked good. I've received flattering comments whenever I wear it.

It was kind of interesting to see that many homos in such a small area. Now when I think back on the dance though, I certainly did not feel like I was one of them. When I left I felt about as un-homo as I ever have. I know I will probably never go to one of them again.

A couple days ago I called the Twin Cities gay chat line if you can believe it! It took me forever to get the courage to do it.

"Hello."

"Hi who's this?"

"Justin."

"You got Jim here."

"Ah, so what are you up to?"

"I'm pretty horny. You?"

"Not a whole lot."

"So how old are you?"

"How old do I sound?"

"24 . . . 25 . . . 26 . . . 27 . . . 28 . . . 29?"

"No."

"23 . . . 22 . . . 21 . . . 20?"

"Ah hahahahaha . . . I'm 17."

"So you just came out."

"And you?"

"Well, I'm old enough to be your father."

(What a turn on - *not*) "So have you found anyone?"

"No, not yet. Well, I suppose you'd be lookin' for someone your own age."

"Yeah . . ."

"Yeah . . ."

I hung up and died laughing. I still haven't called back and I probably never will.

On the way home Mom bluntly asked if I was gay. I said, "No, but does that matter?"

"No, I just want you to know you can feel comfortable and I'm not going to kick you out of the house or anything."

Last Saturday I was at the studio like usual. So was Aiden, that's his name. I bought him a Sprite and went back and talked to him. He called me at night. He asked what we should talk about. I let him choose. He chose sex as the topic. So for two hours we discussed sex.

He's 6 3/4 inches long. Ah, finally a good dick size. I told him flat out that I liked him. I'm so fucking desperate. I want Aiden and I want him now.

I couldn't be more fucked. I got home from going out to a performance art piece on the LA riots to find my mom has found one of the gay pornos I was borrowing from Dwayne.

I was copying the tape in my room so I had both VCRs set up. I came into my room and found the one VCR with the labeled porn tape gone.

I can't find the tape so I figure it's with the VCR, in mom's room.

I go upstairs, get some milk, let the dog out. I go in and kiss her. I notice she has the VCR. I don't say anything. I leave. I get the dog. I wander around. I go back into her room and ask her where the tape is. She says on the VCR. I get it. I leave.

It's *Kramer vs. Kramer*. I got the wrong damn tape.

I go back in and she says it must be IN the VCR. I get it. She says, "Would you like to explain that tape?" I say, "I don't think so." I kiss her again. As I'm leaving she says, "Some weird people on that tape." I laugh and say, "I told you I was copying a tape." Then I say something about how the performance piece was so-so, and leave.

Yesterday was the most surreal day probably of my life. Sam, Steve, Aiden, and I all went to a large playground and soccer field behind South High. I knew something was up when I saw that it was a soccer field. Aiden has a soccer player fetish. I personally, find the Northwest Airlines baggage handlers to be the most attractive people.

It was about 1:40ish AM, we went far out into the center of the field. Then somehow we started giving piggyback rides. Then Aiden, while on Sam's back, attacked me—trying to kiss me! I did kiss Aiden. First on the cheek. Then we actually kissed with our lips. Yes. You read it here, my first kiss ever with another boy happened while he was on my ex-friend's back.

Aiden wanted me to lick his ear. He has small ears. Really sick stuff. Then we collapsed to the ground. "Do you want to go?" He said.

"Yes."

He hopped up, he put his arm in mine and we walked to the car leaving Sam and Steve.

We went back to my house. He didn't want to go home yet. He wanted me to put in a porno so I did—"Malibu Pool Boys." I asked him if it bothered him having my arm on his side. It didn't. And that was how we stayed until 4AM when he went home.

All I ever wanted was someone to hold and I got it. But just that one night was all I got.

THE ART OF LOVE

Lorelei Hill Butters

Least Likely to . . . Win the Caldecott Medal

Growing up, I was the product of divorce, raised by a single mother who didn't exactly have the best taste in men. I, on the other hand, had excellent taste and quickly set my sights on *the* most popular boy in junior high, Lawrence. I should also mention that I had body dysmorphic disorder . . . but in the reverse. I was skinny, awkward, and unpopular, but I thought I was *gorgeous*. People just couldn't see it for some reason.

As a latchkey kid with a lot of time on my hands, I spent much of this time thinking about Lawrence and how to join my life with his. If I got him, I figured everything else in my life would fall into place: All of my problems would go away; all my dreams would come true.

My quest to be with Lawrence didn't just inspire me to write in my diary. It also inspired me to draw a very "hopeful" version of reality.

September 15, 1984
D.D.
Well how are ya? I feel great! I have a new hairstyle.
And a new style of eyeliner. I look like this.

Lawrence Ocon. Wow! I love him! He's the perfect guy except for he's sort of a sosche. Lots of sosche girls like him.

ADULT ME SAYS:

This was my poorly spelled reference to "soc," which was S. E. Hinton's term for upperclass kids in *The Outsiders*.

Especially this girl named Jennifer. She's real ugly! Here's a picture that's really exaggerated but she *is* ugly. She looks like this.

Well back to Larry: Every time I see him I get the chills!

October 10, 1984

My stupid mother has gone and gotten engaged to an asshole! My mother's frenz even laugh in her face when she shows them pictures of him. He is disgusting! He lives on a farm 200 miles away and wants a family. Well fuck him. He ain't getting us! Perhaps she'll find out what a first class schmuck he is and leave him.

About the school newspaper, well I put in a song dedication to Lawrence. It went like this:

TO: Lawrence Ocon. "Stuck on You"
FROM: "Still Waiting."
I guess it stirred up old feelings towards him. Like when we were on the same softball team and he'd pitch and I'd bat. I'll never forget the pride in his face when I made that ball fly. God, I love him.

October 14, 1984
D.D.
Well, I'm "still waiting." God I love Lawrence. I would gladly give myself to him. If I was going with him and it meant keeping him, I would. 14 or 44. Right now if we had a r-thigubithiger or something.

ADULT ME SAYS:

This word was my coded language for "rubber."

I wouldn't want to get pregnant. I don't want to have a baby at 14! I'm sure. I can't afford to have an abortion at my age. Then everyone hates you and talks behind your back. Even people you don't even know!

Lawrence I love you. And whether or not you know it, you love me too. You'll come to me some day and we'll be 2-gether . . . forever.

Visualization is imperative to willing one's future, so here was my first stab at drawing our inevitable happiness.

You'll notice a very tricky dance move in the adjacent image. As a testament to my skills as a choreographer, I'd like to share that this predated *Dirty Dancing* by years.

Monday, Nov. 8, 1984 - 4:00pm

He (my mother's boyfriend) got us an apartment. But it's not for long. He wants to move to Green Valley, he's even selling his ranch. One more thing about him, he hates "niggers." I like them! But he's always talking about how he hates "niggers." I hate him! And hope never to see him again!!

I saw Lawrence today, but briefly. He hopped over the lunch fence to pick something up. It was funny how he can just use one arm to elevate his whole body. God, I swear he can do absolutely no wrong with me! Kim says I'd probably even be impressed with the way he goes to the bathroom! Well, today WAS WEIRD!

January 26, 1984

D.D.

Well I would like very much to have Lawrence to be the first one. You know for what! How should I go about asking him?! This would make a great miniseries! "The only thing she ever wanted was the only man she could never have." I would call it *An Uncrossable Bridge*.

ADULT ME SAYS:

Then I realized that I should not focus on what I didn't have with my Lawrence, but to refocus on what I was determined to have with him.

Lawrence! Here's what I hope to happen with Larry . . .

OUR HOUSE. "I love it!"

ADULT ME SAYS:

While relationships were blossoming in my fantasy life, things back home were taking a different turn.

February 3, 1984

Dear Diary,

Well so much has happened I don't know where to start.

Firstly, mom's NOT getting married! Yay! She says there's just a problem. Like a while ago my mom made a 12lb turkey for him, she even took the day off work to cook it. And he calls up 1 hour after he was supposed to be here and he goes "I'm too tired babe." So she got mad at that! Then 2 weeks later, it's off. Yay!

Lawrence supposedly likes some girl named Nicky. We're friends and that's part of the problem. All 3 of us sit near each other in English. And he talks to her, not me. Plus he put the moves on her last night at the football game! I was really PO'd. Later . . . she said to HIM . . .

Nicky: Do you know Lori?

Larry: Yeah, she's liked me for 3 years now.

Nicky: Well, then what's the problem?

Larry: I don't really know her.

Wow, like he even gives it a chance to know me!

One day when we're married or going, he'll read this diary with me in his arms and he'll say, "Gosh Lori, I love you so much now. How could I have been so blind?"

Then, he'll kiss me. And then, who knows, maybe we'll make love or something.

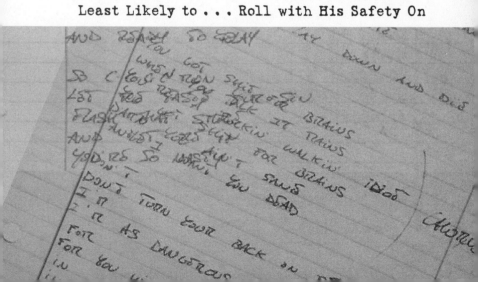

INTRODUCING LIVE EVIL
Laurent Martini
Least Likely to . . . Roll with His Safety On

I was launched to sink. I was short and fat and had braces and huge glasses. My desperate desire to be cool was most likely only surpassed by my extreme desire to have a girlfriend. Knowing that my looks put me at an insurmountable disadvantage, I decided that the only way to achieve my goal was to become a rock star and form the greatest metal band ever: LIVE EVIL.

My love of Mötley Crüe drove me to pen close to one hundred songs, as I desperately tried to evoke the rocker lifestyle: loose women, boozing, and life on the road. The only drawbacks? My upper-middle-class upbringing in the San Francisco Marina District, elite private French schooling, and the fact that I was too lazy to actually form the band.

But I was undeterred. My songs would make me cool. My songs would land me a girlfriend. They were the only chance I had.

I began my quest by writing the kind of cock rock anthem that, according to my research of MTV, seemed to really attract the ladies. Namely, the kind of song that called them horny sluts.

SWEET LITTLE MISSY
Got dirty thoughts
My sweet little missy

Wish I was here
So I could play
With my baby

She does things
Man you wouldn't believe
When you're with her
Wonder if you'll live

She'll let you taste
The original sin
Flash a smile
And let you in
Ho she's so tasty
Sweet little missy

She got an angel's face
And the devil's thoughts
Uses her body
To get her way
Sweet n' tasty
And ready to play

S c-c-c-c-c'mon
Let me taste your sin
Flash that smile
And let me in
You're so nasty
My my my my my my missy

SOLO

No
It ain't never enough
I need some more
It ain't never enough

38

Don't show me the door
It ain't never enough
You know what I'm here for

S-s-s-s-ssweet
So come on
Let me taste your sin
Flash that smile
Let me in

Take me to heaven
N' ring my bell
Let's go down down down
Down to hell
Sweet

Sweet
Sweet
Sweet little missy

ADULT ME SAYS:

Surprisingly, that didn't work. So I decided next to impress
the cool kids. If I could somehow convince the cool kids
that I knew what it was like to be cool, they would invite
me to their parties. Undoubtedly I would meet girls at these
parties and finally have a woman.

BLAME IT ON THE BOOZE
Me and the boys
Were lookin for some action
All the fine ones were gone
We were close to desperation
So we took the ugly girls

And went on our way
If we have any trouble
We'll just have to say

CHORUS

Blame it on the booze
Cause I ain't guilty
Blame it on the booze
Ain't you sorry that you trusted me?
You've got to
Blame it on the booze baby

Long legs and sexy
In her lingerie
Screamin' "Do me! Do me!
Everyway"

Little did she know
That I thought she was ugly
I was just fucking her
My own private party

CHORUS

Now when I'm sober
She really makes me sick
But a dose of alcohol
Always does the trick

She looks better
After every shot
And if we were together
I'd do her on the spot

CHORUS

Sadly, the cool kids were less than impressed with a song about getting ugly girls drunk to fuck them. So I decided to try to impress the girls again. This time I would write a ballad. Of course, Live Evil was not just going to write any sappy love song. If Live Evil was going to write a rock ballad, it was going to have to still kick ass. And it was going to be about drinking.

My friend and I used to get drunk by drinking Jack Daniel's. Straight. Because it gave me heartburn, I switched to Baileys. Which I also drank. Straight. But even I knew that wasn't cool, so I wrote a song called:

SHOT OF JACK
I need a shot of whiskey
A shot of Jack
Feel so lonely
Got to get this bitch off of my back

So I hop a freight train
I'm heading home
Seen so much pain
Where ever I may roam

So I play my guitar
I trust it well
She's never lied
You know this life is livin' hell

Give me a shot of Jack
When all is wrong

Heart attack
Want to be real fucking gone

You know I'm on the run
Against the law
I've got to do it
Dirty, live and raw

You know they'd sell your soul
Just for a dime
For the devil's money
They would do just any crime

So give me a shot of whiskey
A shot of Jack
I'm still lonely
And this bitch still on my back

A shot of Jack
When all is wrong
Off the tracks
Heartbeat's almost gone

ADULT ME SAYS:

Strike three. Not only did no one believe the intense
emotional pain in the song, no one cared. I tried to get a
girlfriend. And failed. I tried to impress the cool kids. And
failed. What was I to do? The only thing that any artist does
when their back is against the wall, that's what! They create
their greatest piece, their swan song, their *Sgt. Pepper's*.
And my *Sgt. Pepper's* was called:

SHIT FOR BRAINS

I
I'm a social disgrace
I
I'd like to spit in your face
You
You think you're so grand
I
I don't think you'll stand
You
With your suit and tie
I
I'd rather lay down and die
Than be
Like you

CHORUS

You got shit for brains
When you talk it rains
You're a fuckin walkin idiot
You got shit for brains
When you talk it rains
You're a fuckin walkin idiot
You got shit for brains

Don't
Don't turn your back on me
I'm
I'm as dangerous as can be
For
For you will die tonight
In
In this switchblade fight
I
I'll knock you out

In
In this heavyweight bout
So just
Fuck you

CHORUS

TALK: hey man, take it all to heart
Cause if you've been affected by what I said
Then you're one of those fuckers
Who's always on my case
So listen up
And listen good
FUCK YOU

ADULT ME SAYS:

I eventually got a girl. But not as a rock star. As an antiques
dealer. We married. Then divorced.

And now that I'm back to where I began in some ways,
I find myself whistling Live Evil anthems in my head,
listening for the sound of screaming fans as I check the
office answering machine.

GOOD CHEER

Sherry Richert Belul

Most Spirited

I was a cheerleader all throughout high school in the Midwest. After graduation I went away to college, to a university in Indiana, about eight hours away.

My sophomore year I started getting calls from the man who had been the high school football coach when I'd been cheerleading for the football team. He was twenty-eight when he started calling, and I had just turned nineteen. I was a virgin. He wasn't.

This is the story of the romance that ensued.

Nov. 29th, 1983
At 6:15 I got a call. It was Luke Castelli from Maplewood!!!!! I answered the phone and he said, "Sherry this is Luke Castelli from Maplewood." First it popped into my mind that someone died. Then he said he used to be a football coach, and I thought perhaps there was a special banquet!! But it turns out, he just wants to meet me. I am really flattered.

He said he used to watch me cheerleading and he'd always tell the other coaches what a cute girl I was. Said he's never done this before. I was flabbergasted. He looked up my number and called.

He told me that he's the head coach at a different school now. But he added that he isn't that old, just

47

had a lot of lucky breaks. I'm intrigued. Totally. He said he'd call again. I'm excited. I'm just tickled pink.

Dec. 4th, 1983

Luke called again! We talked about so many things. He's into honesty as much as I am! I really feel like I could fall for him. He asked if I was still tiny and pretty. And we talked about what he looks like. He told me he's 28, older than I thought. He said he wants it to be forever when he marries. That when he's 70 he can go to the mall with his wife and hold hands. I love that!!!! I feel the same way.

Dec. 16th, 1983

Luke called! We made plans to get together. He got here and I didn't know what to think. He talked a lot to my mom. They talked about our musical Christmas cards that wouldn't shut up and about his pet snake.

I remember getting to his house and looking around and seeing all of the basketball/football stuff. He got us some wine (in Los Angeles Rams glasses). Already I felt like I knew Luke. He even kissed me. We decorated the tree. He pulled me down next to him and we talked about whether we usually make love with people on the first date. I said, "I don't at all."

He said he never thought we'd make love. Never crossed his mind. He ended up picking me up and taking me into his bedroom. He kept saying how pretty and sweet I was. He talked about coming to visit me at school.

I like that he likes me. I was disappointed in the
fake fireplace, though.

Dec. 17th, 1983

I felt chipper. Luke got here and we ended up just
driving and driving. He told me so much about
himself. How he had bad grades in high school and
had to cheat to get into college. He told me why he
chose teaching—because he wanted to be a coach!
Funny how this all didn't make me look down on
him. We stopped for coffee and he told me all about
his first year as a coach. About how they won a game
they were supposed to get creamed in. The things
he does to psych the team up. He is so thoughtful. I
really enjoy hearing him talk.

On the way home he sung "The Last Game of
the Season." He's so mushy. We sat on his bed to read
football articles and he started kissing me. He told me
Mr. B had described me as "top shelf"—you know,
like they put all the best whiskey on the top shelf. We
laughed because he uses so many analogies.

ADULT ME SAYS:

I doubt Luke even knew what an analogy was.

Dec. 18th, 1983

At Luke's house again. Luke and I ended up together
as usual. But then things got to be too much again.
He rolled over and wouldn't talk. Then he said he was

49

hurt. You wouldn't think sex could be such a major obstacle would you?

He asked how many kids I wanted to have and if I would consider a relationship with someone older. He said he thought about me for two years and I'm like a car he doesn't need to test drive more than once.

Dec 19th, 1983

Luke is so much fun. On the way to his house he told me about all the cars he has owned. He was kind of drunk and feeling chipper. Kept calling me Goob. I asked Luke if he had ever seen the play, *Scrooge*. He said he isn't very cultured or refined. Then we talked about his favorite color and whether he likes donuts. He wondered if I lived here if things would become "forever."

He compared us to a game "you go into knowing you're going to dominate." He told me that he'd like to hold my hand in the mall.

Dec 23rd, 1983

Luke called and asked me to breakfast. He told me we were going to Bob Evans. Yay! I was so thrilled. I got fried mush. He ate a waffle and a "side of egg." We talked on and on about the Bob Evans in Richmond, Indiana. He's been there. Twice! He called me a goober and smooched me goodbye. I think I really do love him.

Dec 27th, 1983

Well. This is it, kiddo. I made love. Who would
have guessed? The world didn't explode and I didn't
even cry. I don't feel any different at all. We had been
kissing on his bed after looking at the yearbook. Then
things got going and we were together. I hardly knew.
It felt good, but I still wasn't sure if this was it. For
some reason I didn't know if he was all in. Luke didn't
say much.

I had three slow gin fizzes at Gordon's. Billy Joel
was on and we played Yahtzee. It was cozy in the
kitchen and they joked about my butt. It all felt so
romantic. I liked the thought that I would remember
this scene whenever I thought back on the night I first
made love.

Jan 23rd, 1984

Luke and I talked tonight and he said something
about "two more years of this." Which makes me
think he plans on sticking with me. He talked about
us eloping and living in the mountains. I said I
wished we could go to Denny's.

Feb 5th, 1984

We made love but Luke's stomach hurt. I was
disappointed we weren't going for breakfast. We
just lay there. I couldn't bear the thought of leaving
him. I cried over everything. But then we stopped at
Lawson's and I felt bad because he bought me a bagel.
I felt spoiled. He said he understood that I get all mad

because I have to leave. He gave me potato chips for
the car ride. It's so great to love him.

Feb 11th, 1984
I wish Luke would call. I do love him. I'm scared
though. I can't be #2 in someone's life and I'm afraid I
would be with him. Football means so much to him.

Feb 28th, 1984
Luke called to apologize for last night. Whew. But
then we talked for about 20 minutes and it wasn't
good. He talked about how we can't get too involved
while I'm away. And how we shouldn't have made
love and how he knows we'll be together someday.
He insinuated that I'm bored here and that's why I
miss him. Said he's going out with other girls and he
hopes I know. I cried and cried afterward. I think it is
ending.

March 8th, 1984
Luke didn't call. I'm so sad. Sat and cried. What is
there now? I listened to "Got to Be There" (Michael
Jackson) and cried. I felt better. But then I listened to
Simon and Garfunkel and got sad again.

March 18th, 1984
I'm obsessed with Luke. God, I miss him so much. I
was thinking of playing Yahtzee at Gordon's and how
fun it was. Thinking of Ho-Ho's and fruit pies in the
morning. Even after all the shit, I do love him.

This is a poem I wrote him to feel some sort of closure. I tried to use language he might understand. There were actually about twenty-five stanzas, but I thought I'd spare you all of them.

Stranger now the game is done.
None kept score so who has won?
I guess we both did, in a way
For now there's more games we can play.

Stranger I could play a little more.
But you're not happy unless you score.
And with the weather so unclear
You won't even run, because of fear.

Stranger it was great, though tough.
But whoever said the game isn't rough?
And whoever said it is all in the score
I guess the fun is what playing is for.

MY LIFE AS A BIKER BABE
Jane Cantillon

Most Likely to . . . Flash a Priest

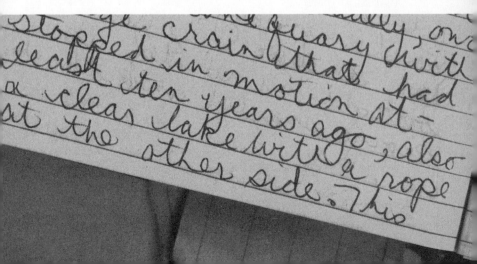

I was a wild Catholic-school girl, deeply into the spin-the-bottle circuit of early-1970s Cleveland. But that life just wasn't cutting it. So by the time I was sixteen, I started hanging with an older crowd—the kind with wisdom, life experience, and fringed leather jackets. The reason was Bear, the love of my life back then and a proud member of the Hells Angels.

It was the height of biker culture. Post–*Easy Rider*. Post-Altamont. Pre-Fonzie. And it was the height of my love for him.

December 20, 1973

I'd better summarize "the latest" before this year comes to a close! If I haven't mentioned it, I got starved for romance so I started seeing Bear after his first phone call. His Harley Davidson drove me wild in excitement and stimulation. He seemed extroverted and aggressive at first.

I met all of his decadent friends, such as Scrounge, a real primate biker who has a true cave man voice and attitude. Woodrow, a biker who looks like he just jumped out of the woods. George, a girl who had the factory job. Her eyes are weak and they cross to the middle. Skunk is a biker who has half

57

black/brown, half white hair and talks, acts, and sometimes smells like a skunk. Greg is a nice Italian biker with big piercing blue eyes and a fox-like hairline. He reminded me of Sam the Sham.

Bear picked me up from school wearing his deer skin vest and looking so Bearish on his big red sparkled Harley. Only the freshmen could be appalled. Our dates were rides in the country usually. It was all very romantic but he didn't touch me until we were zooming home did he suggest "Let's have a little sex." All I could scream was "It's about time!"

Bear got a night shift job circuiting torpedoes (phallic job of the century!) My telephone soliciting job was great. Our boss was my favorite. He is a promotion man from LA, doing this for Junior Chamber of Commerce. Actually, he had to leave the coast cause cocaine was fixed in his brain.

I used to go to Val's and hang out in the parking lot with the bikers, smoke dope, and watch Bear become doctor of the Bikes. The Bikers always treated me like such a fine woman, complete respect. Especially when we hung out in the Grand Prix. One time I got to sit in the luxury liner with Bear's friend Geoff Christian (a perfect WASP), John (a boy who is missing half of his front teeth), and some other biker. We listened to *Clockwork Orange* music while they compared switchblades and we smoked dope.

I met some more interesting people I would like to remember. 1st Janet—a black girl who was raped and her car was stolen about a year ago. She got gonorrhea and didn't know it. It ruined her ovaries and left her temporarily paralyzed. Her parents went mad and they have sheltered her to mental sterility almost.

Now she is waiting for her boyfriend to return from somewhere and she has a business agreement with Bruce to ease her horniness with frequent sexual activities. She doesn't know him well but she feels it is important to use someone who you feel can pull the emotional from the physical, yet still look down as a superior!? She was very naïve about the hardened world, though not afraid.

We went to Val's and I was a brat as ever to poor lonesome Bear. I met this girl he knows who was short, blond, and bubbly, with a nice husky round body, white skin, and a small mouth with sweet red lips. Her name was Brandy (but the Angels call her "Lady".) She lives in San Francisco but just split up with her Hell's Angels beau named Patches whom she was going with for 3 years. She started telling me about her relatives who were bikers. She has 13 brothers so she doesn't fuck around. She has a long sharp switchblade she carries beside her muscle-bound bicep. Her mother was a French Gypsy. I asked her to just babble some French to me. She babbled like a French floozy— beautifully.

Then she started talking about her being bisexual,

and she wanted to show me some pictures her "bitches" took just to show me what kind of tricks they do, but I smoothly pulled myself out of that proposition. Her girlfriend was an example of a lovely death warmed over, with a smile like a mad woman and a green tinted face. When I said goodbye to Brandy, she gave me 3 warm kisses goodbye, almost adorning kisses, and left a sweet scent on my hair.

Bear and I had another date visiting his friend in the hospital who had just gotten his leg amputated in a bike crash (next to Bear.) While I was in the room, "Stumpy" (new nickname) started accusing Bear for the accident. The tension was mind blowing along with Skunk and Woodrow in the room questioning the facts of fault. This was our last date.

When I look back, so much has happened. I've found out more about myself. I feel sorry for people too easily, and take people too seriously. Everyday I find more about myself. This month, I think I could of had a nervous breakdown if I wanted it. Uh oh, I'm getting tired, better sign off.

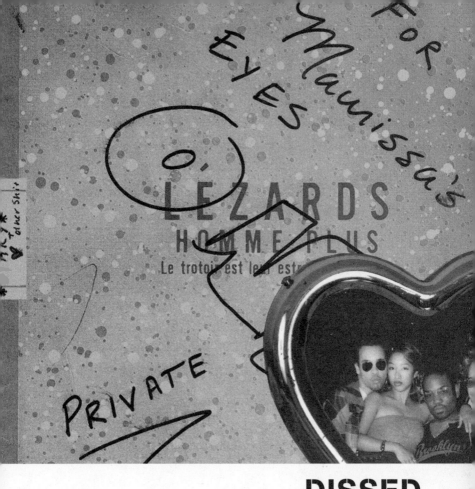

FOR Maurissas EYES O, ONLY

LEZARDS
HOMME PLUS
Le trotoir est leur estr

PRIVATE

DISSED
Maurissa Tancharoen
Least Likely to . . . Be in Politics

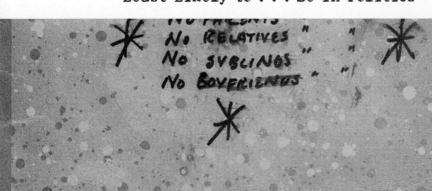

NO PARENTS "
No RELATIVES " "
No SIBLINGS " "
No BOYFRIENDS " "

I grew up the very good little Asian girl. I went to private school, studied hard, and got good grades. I had a set schedule of after-school activities, from piano lessons to ballet lessons.

Then puberty hit, and I suddenly had a problem with being Asian. I started hanging out with a new crowd. I walked differently and talked differently. I listened to nothing but hip-hop and R&B. I basically tried to be a completely different person, all attitude.

By fifteen I was dating one of the hottest seniors in high school. So, no bullshit, I wrote this as "the girl I thought I was" back in the day.

Just got home. It's Friday night. Bobby and I went pretty far tonight. I don't know if this is good. I didn't let him go down there, but he did SUCK ON MY BOOBS. Oh man, I hope nobody finds this.

What should I do? I can't believe he had the nerve to say to me, "When I can have allllll dis, I'll be a happy guy." What a jerk! That makes me feel yuck! I need to . . . talk to him . . . tell him how I feel! Write him a note! Be straight up!!! I need to set his ass straight. Fa real doh. This is what I'll put in the note.

Bobby,

I thought about what happened last night and I don't feel too good about it. I ain't never moved that fast before. I mean, do you really like me? Or do you just want to do it to me? It's only been two weeks. What did you expect from me? I don't get down like that. Okay? Shoot.

And I am sick of people telling me things. Catching you talking to other girls. Talk to ME. Hello?! You hardly ever call me. Or page me.

You don't seem interested in my family. You don't care that I know how to play Chopin, or that I can do a double-pirouette! That is *all* part of me Bobby!

Maybe it's just too soon. All you seem interested in is how far you can go wit me. I ain't no Angela! Gross.

If you really like me, you would be concerned . . . ask permission . . . show respect.

Not just suck on them! I mean, it felt good but it didn't feel good after. If sex is allll you want, then we might as well call it quits now 'cause pretty soon yo gonna get fed up with me saying "no" cause that's what I'ma do!!! I ain't no fool, Bobby!

Unless we're madly in love and we've been committed for a long period of time, then MAYBE I'll be down for it.

Straight up?? I don't even know why I let you go that far, sucking my boobs.

I mean, you dated people like Angela. She is a total HO! Everybody in school has did it to her.

Okay?! My last boyfriend was my first boyfriend ever and he's in a cereal commercial doing the running man! Which is totally dope! And he still wants to be with me, F.Y.I. But all we ever did was kiss! And I was fine with dat.

Look, all I'm saying is, I know you're a senior, and you're experienced and you could get with girls yo age, but you picked me for a *reason*. So think about that reason Bobby. Think about it good. And call me. Peace out,

Maurissa

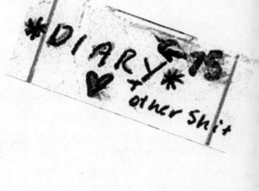

report. I just wanted to
to say hi and say some
I guess... well First
week was awesome!! It
was,,,,,,,, we started it off
a bang. The night I gave
massage started
on the right Fo
perfect,... the co
oyz II MEN pumpin
wnted it to be
hoogh it was jus

THE PUSSY-WHIPPED PLAYA
Charles Young
Most Likely to . . . Be Like James Van Der Beek in DAWSON'S CREEK

the little Mermaid was
and bubba's ruled, I
love hanging out with
I love knowing that
e by my side, I
l you there,,,,,, I
need you, I want you

When I was young, I treated my girlfriends like *shit*. I'd like to say that it was because I was thirteen and didn't know any better. But I think it was because I could. Prepubescent Chuck thought he was the shit, and the ladies weren't telling him any different.

Then puberty struck—pimples rose, chubbiness appeared, and desolation took confidence's place. Meanwhile, all the girls around me blossomed and became beautiful women ripe for the picking of older guys.

As I sank into depression, I began reflecting on the way I had treated girls. I saw high school seniors scoop them up and treat them terribly, and I vowed in my loneliness that if I were to get another girlfriend, *I'd treat her like gold.*

I got that girlfriend at sixteen. What follows are letters I wrote to her in a journal *she bought for us.* I was trying to say the things I thought a boyfriend would say, while still trying to keep some kind of badass vibe. I was like a total pussy who listened to Dr. Dre's *The Chronic* record on repeat.

11/9/1997

I took a shower tonight and the only light I had was the light from a candle. It was beautiful. Looking out through the glass doors of my shower and seeing just the beautiful flicker of a candle. It made me think of you. Whenever I see something beautiful I think of you. To me, beauty equals you. You are everything. You are everything that is beautiful . . . You're sexy in my dreams but even sexier in real life. Hug me, kiss me, love me.

You're retarded boyfriend,
Chuck

11/14/1997

Hi there sweetheart! This journal thing rules. I wish you were with me last night. the show was rad but it's just so much radder when the love of my life is there. I also want to say sorry for yesterday. I don't think that I was a hootch to you personally, but I was just generally a hootch because of my tiredness and my malnutrition. Talk to you later. Keep smiling . . . Always remember . . . I love you.

11/25/1997

Massage today, well . . . almost tonight. I'm working today but after I'd like to hook up a mean massage session for you and then you can leave and do whatever or we can both leave and do something or what not . . . I got the best meditation idea thing too so be prepared for that. Just tell me what's up, if you want a massage or what not . . .

Do me a favor . . . don't dwell in the shitty stuff I said. I AM retarded but I don't know why. Things are getting better, maybe slowly but we're getting

there . . . or i'm getting there. I have a lot of issues I
have to deal with. Me and you are the shit though,
pumpkin ass, and don't you forget that . . . ever.
Much love, homey
Peace

11/30/1997

Hey sweetheart,
Sorry I can't write for too long. . . . I still have to do
a stupid report. I just wanted to write to say hi and
say some things I guess . . . Well, first this week was
awesome! It really was . . . we started it off with a
bang. The night I gave you a massage started the week
off on the right foot. It was perfect . . . the candles
blazin', the boyz to men pumpin' . . . you. I wanted
it to be special even though it was just a massage. I
thought it was romantic and I thought we could use a
little romance. Then *The Little Mermaid* was cool and
Bubba's ruled. I just love hanging out with you. I
love knowing that you're by my side. I need you
there . . . I just need you. I want you . . . I don't know
why I just said that . . . I guess I'm a hornball!

   Just kidding. I do want you though . . . pretty bad
but that's a different story all together but anyway, I
guess I just wanted to say that I love you and I always
will. You're my sunshine. You make the days go by
and don't ever forget that. Alright, see you tomorrow.
I love you . . . nice ass.

12/10/1997

You look so f-in hot today. Your outfit rules! Those pants look so good on you. When I saw you . . . I was all "Damn" and you were all "Right?" and I was all "Right on, sweetie" and so on and so forth. I'm glad you liked the kiss . . . I liked it too. If I kissed you all of the times I wanted to all hell will break loose. Anyway have a good day and I'll see ya.
Love always.

12/19/1997

Tonight I'm relaxing after work . . . probably get some sleep, take a bath, dance to some tunes but most of all, I'll be thinking of my love and waiting for her to call me. i need to see you tonight . . . It feels like we're so far away and I'd love to feel you in my arms. Close to me . . . we keep getting closer and you know that. Sometimes we grow far apart but in doing so we get closer. Let's be rad . . . a rad, styling couple totally in LOVE with each other.
Stay true, sweetheart and keep it real.
Love,
Gangsta

1/5/1998

I'm in love with you . . . so in love. You are my rose . . . (rose as in a beautiful flower and rose as in Rose from *Titanic*). And hopefully some day I can be good enough to be your jack. To be able to save you in every way possible. Me and you are the shit! (for

lack of a better word) and you know that. You're so
beautiful, so sweet, so caring and loving, you make
me laugh, we have fun and we're so comfortable with
each other. I love you.
Chuck
. . . and she responds, "YOU ARE MY JACK, YOU
ALREADY DID SAVE ME."

1/22/1998

I get so fucking mad when I think about stupid
spanish fuckers fucking with you. I want so bad just
go walk up and spit in their faces and tell them off but
I know that'll just make things worse. They'd end up
fucking with you more just to egg me on to violence.
It just gets me so mad. I hate perverted shit especially
when it has to do with you. You, the girl that I'm
totally in love with I don't . . . I just get mad at gross
shit. Weather you say it or it's said to you or you and
someone else are joking around. I just F-in hate it.

1/30/1998

You make me feel so good about everything Nothing
else matters to me but you. I'm so in love with you.
I'm so, so deep in the ocean of love and happiness
that I might drown. We are so alike and we do rule.
Don't ever feel like you have to change. You are the
bomb girl and even though that sounds cheesy and
homeboy, it's the utter truth.

You are the bomb! The bomb that makes my
heart explode with utter devotion, loyalty, happiness,

sweetness and most of all . . . love. I just hope I can be good to you. Fuck good . . . I hope I can and will be the best to you. I love you and it's like a rose . . . except it will not wither and fade away.

Love's the word of the day.

Love's the word.
of the day ♡ ♡ ♡ ♡

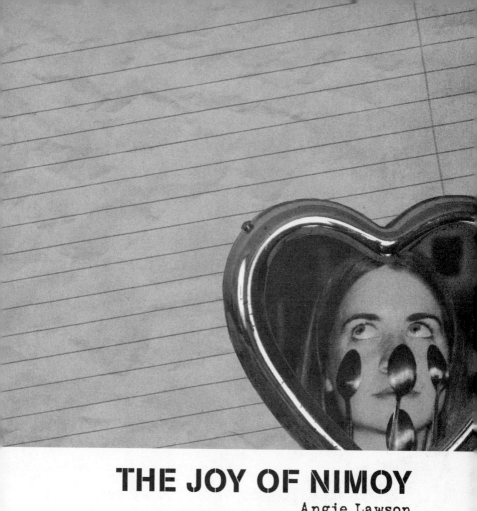

THE JOY OF NIMOY

Angie Lawson

Least Likely to . . . Speak Vulcan

When I was fifteen, they started re-airing episodes of the 1960s TV series *Mission: Impossible*. I watched religiously after school and soon fell madly and hopelessly in love with the great Paris, played by Leonard Nimoy.

Here is the love song I wrote him for his birthday; I have long since forgotten the tune. I was never a "trekkie," so I'm not really sure where all of the Star Trek references came from.

Dearest Leonard,

My name is Angie but my friends call me Angelina Ballerina. I am 16 years old and I think you're swell. I just thought it would be nice to wish you a happy 64th birthday and send you a poem that I had written about you. I am going to bake you a birthday cake and celebrate with my friends and my life size stand up picture of you as Spock. Even though you can't join us in person, I know you'll be there in spirit. I wish the transporter beams had really been invented.

Don't get me wrong, I am not one of those fanatical *Star Trek* fans. I only watch it to catch an occasional glimpse of you. This is also a reason I have become addicted to *Mission Impossible*. Oh well. I will probably never meet you in person. I just wanted

to express for you my undying love. Have a nice
birthday. Live long and prosper.
Love,
Angelina Ballerina

Love's First Name is Leonard
by Angie Lawson (angelina ballerina)

My love spells his name L-E-O-N-A-R-D,
He is my one true love, but has never met me.

My love for him will surely last forever more,
He starred on *Star Trek* beside Shatner (who's a bore).

I know that he is so much more than "Mr. Spock,"
If someday I meet him I will die from the shock.

If I were to meet him, how could I ever say,
That all my life I've dreamt about meeting him
someday?

I've got a lot of pictures of him on the wall,
When I look into his eyes I stumble, and fall.

When he lifts an eyebrow, I can't control myself,
He wears those Vulcan ears and looks just like an elf.

His beautifully striking face fills my heart with joy,
Love's first name is Leonard and its last is Nimoy!

When I was fifteen, I actually tried to mail this to him, but I chickened out.

Friday July 16, 1993
Today, to start OFF
my trip, I woke up
at 3:30 am, and
we left the house by
4:00. There are
nine of us here, and
we are: me, Dad,
Mindy Sherman, Joanna
Kotz, Donna from
Shrewsbury, Colleen &
Shanna from Shrewsbury,
Leonore, who speaks
Spanish, and
Wilson. He
project. I'm
REALLY, w
come to I
Liz, we
a better
and she's Hispani
so she's our translat
then, of course, there
main squeez
alas,

nice, also. She mos
stays to herself. Sh
really pretty, and
jealous. Donna,
but I think
thinks she
the kids. S
queer laugh.
dad is a mu
st
rea

This book belongs to

FOREIGN AFFAIRS
Liz Black

Most Likely to . . . Work in a Soup Kitchen

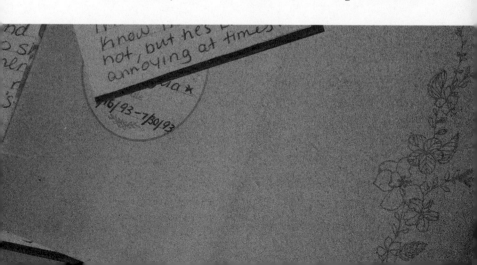

know
not, but he's
annoying at times

7/16/93–7/30/93

The summer after my freshman year of high school, I went on a retreat to Nicaragua with my minister dad and a group of high schoolers. Like me, they had raging hormones and a minimal grasp of the Spanish language. What should have been a spiritual learning experience ended up being more like *Sunday School Girls Gone Wild*.

My love interests on the trip included pretty much every nearby male under the age of twenty-five. But being that I was a forty-year-old trapped in a fourteen-year-old's body, and that I was with my Bible-toting dad, this trip was not the steamy telenovela I secretly craved.

Friday, July 16, 1993

Today to start off my trip, I woke up at 3:30am and we left the house by 4. There are 9 of us here and we are: me, Dad, Mindy, Joanna, Donna, Colleen, Shanna, Leonore who speaks Spanish, and Eric. He is my project. I'll work on it for a while but REALLY, we did not come to find romance, Liz. We came to become a better person.

Colleen and Shanna are a little annoying. They are loud and are always talking. They never shut up. Plus I think they like Eric but I don't have to worry since he and I are buddies anyhow (heh heh, GO LIZ!)

Mindy is really nice. She's making a gift for her boyfriend consisting of a barf bag and whatever she finds here. She brought about 8 million Handi-wipes with her and a ton of toilet paper. She's funny. Joanna is nice also. She's really pretty and I'm jealous. Donna's ok but I think she thinks she's one of the kids. She has a queer laugh. Leonore's dad is a minister and she's Hispanic so she's our translator.

Then, of course, there is my main squeeze. He is so hot. But alas, we did not come here to find love. I think my dad thinks I'm in love with Eric but I'm not. He's hot but kinda annoying at times.

Maybe I'll lose some weight and look just like supermodel Cindy Crawford when I return. Ok Liz, you're queer.

Once we got to the house in Managua we went to a lake. It was wonderful. I can't tell about Eric. He followed me in the lake but he also acted like he liked Shanna and Colleen even though we agreed they were queer. We found pumice stones in the lake too. So at least I'll have very pretty feet while I'm here.

Saturday, July 17
Colleen and Shanna aren't as bad. They are actually pretty nice when they're not talking. I don't like Eric either. Ok, he's hot but annoying! He hasn't shut up.

It's weird to talk entirely in Spanish because I have no idea what I'm doing. Donna is really queer,

she's always sweaty which is gross and she doesn't
shut up.

On the truck today we passed some guy who
made a pass at Shanna (don't ASK me why) and he
followed us on his bike for a mile at least. Then he
made a kissing face at her. It was so funny!

Well, I don't know about you but I'm bushed!
Adios! (No more Spanish, <u>PLEASE</u>!)

annoying at times.

Sunday, July 18

Eric is queer. At the beach he pulled me underwater
and I got all scratched up. I don't like him anymore.
I also don't like Shanna. But Colleen's ok. At church
this morning we sang "Do Lord" and I don't think
they were impressed at all. Unless giving someone
a blank stare here is a compliment. Mindy keeps
singing the *Love Boat* theme.

Today at the beach Ben or John goes to me "Can
I ask you a question?" and so of course I'm like "Of
course your holy hotness!" and he says "Could you
wipe your nose?" I was so embarrassed! I had a huge
booger hanging out! I think they think I'm queer now.

Wednesday, July 21

Ok, I'm freaked out. There is a WAR in this fine old
country I'm staying in. Mindy and I fear for our lives.

We went to the barrio because they scheduled
a basketball game between us and the barrio, but
we ended up playing w/ mixed teams. I didn't have
too good a time although Mindy was on my team,

because I realize that I'm a very stinky basketball player. OH. So THAT'S why nobody passed to me ☺ After, we played Frisbee and kickball. I don't know if it's being in a foreign country or not knowing the language but for some reason I'm not as coordinated as I am in the US of A! Of course, when have I ever been coordinated?

After Frisbee and kickball, we (Mindy + Dad + I) walked to the house where the radio was blaring in Spanish about something. My father asked if I remembered the helicopters we saw flying overhead today in the truck. I said yes but I really only remembered vaguely. He said they weren't on a practice run, they were heading for the northern part of the country. Later, Rosa told me it was war. That was when I got scared.

Thursday, July 22

War's over. I guess you could say it was a quickie. There was nothing on the radio about it today.

I want to be just like Leo when I grow up. She's so organic and she eats all natural stuff and does martial arts and wears dresses all the time and is a masseuse. She's so COOL. Eric is queer. BYE!

Saturday, July 24

After church last night they sold Cokes to everyone. Earlier, we found crates of Coke and were going to help ourselves but they locked them up right after we found them. (There's a jail that's on the island right behind the church.)

Ok, I'm officially grossed out. When Ricky got back today he found a real live scorpion in his BIBLE! I think it's a sign. Luckily we killed it.

Sunday, July 25
Colleen is now Jose's *novia*. It's so sick. And Eric is dating Marsela, one of the girls from the barrio. I think these Nicaraguans should set some standards for themselves. Yikes.

Monday, July 26
Today we went to the beach at Pochomil on the Pacific coast and I found out why Eric was so touchy about his lover girl. They went quite far on their trip, or so Colleen says because she and I took a little walk today and chatted. But then again Colleen and Jose went pretty far too. That makes me quite ill considering they've only known each other a few days. But, whatever they want to do, they'll do.

It was really surprising when everyone from the barrio showed up at the beach, including the lovers and it was SICK. They were making out all over the beach in front of everyone and I wanted to just go up to Ricky and tell him that not all kids are that, shall we say, FRISKY. But no one cared. Mindy and I spent the whole time making fun of Eric. Such a geek.

Tuesday, July 27
When we got home tonight we had dinner and Leo and Mindy and Colleen and I talked about guys. I

stayed out of the talking part and just took everything in, considering I don't have much to contribute in that subject.

Wednesday, July 28

Went to Masaya volcano today and we stood at the top. It was a very long stairclimb to the top. (Exercise! Nordic Track!) Rick asked for any sacrifices to throw into the volcano and I said I'd go. What the hey, you only live once. :) It was fun.

Thursday, July 29

LAST REAL DAY HERE! I'm gonna miss everyone. I know I wanted to come home the whole time I've been here and I still do, but I'm not as excited to <u>leave</u> as I first was. Remember: You don't always have to speak the same language and laughing is universal.

Friday, July 30

I'm finally home. On the plane I unfortunately had to sit next to you know who again (Eric), then we went through customs in Miami (no bags got dumped out but dumb old Shanna couldn't find her passport or entrance papers). Everyone was at the airport: Mindy's family, Joanna's whole family, my whole family. Everyone! It was great.

1623rd (Friday)
I can't stand to face it.
now we're through forever
I keep telling myself the
it's just a bad dream + I ji
+ I'll wake
be okay +
again. If
n't went
o on living

COWGIRL
Lucinda Blackwood
Most Likely to . . . Get Engaged

+ take me back, just
it was before. Exactl
'aip ago he said told me
oved me "but I wouldn'
e him if only I'd given

In my hometown, the stretch of Main Street between Piggly Wiggly and the Wildcat Drive-In offered all the promise of fun and romance a teenager could hope for. On the Texas–New Mexico border, surrounded by oil wells, cattle ranches, and mesquite trees, it was easy for a young girl to fall prey to the allure of a "bad boy" in tight jeans and dirty boots.

My pink leather diary was inscribed with the name "Dale" on every inch of its outside and inside covers. It was 1968. I was fifteen years old. Not only was I in love with love, I was in love with *cowboys* and *country music*. I dreamed of a wedding that involved both. Little did I know, just like in the words of a country song I was about to be stepped on, lied to, cheated on, and treated like dirt.

May 31

I had a date with Dale tonight. He picked me up at 6:00 pm and we went to get a Coke, drug Main, went to the rodeo grounds, drug Main, went over to Danny's house. He wasn't home, back to rodeo grounds, left, drug, went back, talked to Lumpy and his wife. I stayed with her while Dale got ready and rode bareback bronc. He didn't qualify!!!!

June 13

Oh gosh! I told Dale I loved him for the first time tonight. I think I do and he said he loves me "a little bit." He says he's confused because of a girl that lives in the upper part of the state! I love him so much, I wish he loved me half as much as I love him, then that would be a hell of a lot!

June 14

DALE

June 15

DALE

June 16, June 17, June 18, June 19

DALE DALE DALE DALE

June 20

Waited ALL DAY for "ASS" to call. NEVER DID!

August 21

Went to the parade. Saw Dale at Ole Jax with a girl piled in with him! Went over to the rodeo about 7:00. Dale rode in the Grand Entry. He was an absolute ASS! Stayed at the rodeo awhile, then just before we left Dale comes walking up with some girl. He saw me and the look on his face was UNBELIEVABLE. He looked like somebody just slapped him in the face with a cold rag or something and he just turned and herded that girl off. I've NEVER felt that way in my life! I love, love, love Dale and he does not love me anymore, I just know it. Oh! Dale.

August 22
I took down all my "Dale" stuff for the very last time.

August 23
I know we're through forever, but I keep telling myself this is all just a bad dream. Exactly ten days ago he told me he loved me, but I wouldn't believe him. If only I'd given in and accepted it as the truth. It's repulsive to feel sorry for myself, but don't I have a reason?! Well, tonight I'll see Dale again. He won't speak. He'll be with some girl, treating her like he used to treat me. And I thought I was special to him, but I was so wrong. Please Dale, love me again.

September 4
I was in bed just about to cry my fool self to sleep and the phone rang. I just knew it was Susan and she had called to let me hear some sad song on the radio, but when I answered DALE said, "What are you doing?" and I was NEVER so happy in my life. I don't think I'd have made it through last night if it hadn't been for him calling. I told him I loved him for the first time since about the 7th of August and it felt good to say it again. I wouldn't tell him last week, my stupid pride wouldn't let me, but now I don't give a damn about my pride, it doesn't mean anything when it comes to loving Dale. I hope he knows that and won't take

advantage of it and treat me like he did before, again. No one knows how much I really love Dale, not even Susan. I love him as much as anything else in the world, maybe even more and that's a lot!

September 5
Today at the "Wildcat" Dale was precious. Oh, he was cute. Better than that, ADORABLE! He picked me up tonite about 7:15. We went ridin' around. We were sittin' in the car and Dale took off his Senior ring and put it on my finger and said "OK?" I didn't say anything—I couldn't! He said he's wanted to ask me so many times but kept thinking of excuses not to all summer. Oh, his ring is beautiful and I'm so happy I could just bust wide open. This was the HAPPIEST Day of My Life!

September 6
Dale picked me up for school. OH OH OH it was cool. I was waiting and the first thing he wanted to do was . . . kiss me, and I wouldn't let him . . . all morning! Damn I love that guy so much!

September 7
Dale hasn't called and I'm plenty mad. Oh. He's had it! OOOHHH! Why do I love him? I don't really know. I'VE HAD IT WITH DALE—THRU!!

September 8
I'm still THRU THRU THRU with DALE FOREVER

September 9
I'm just as through as yesterday.

September 10
Dale finally called. We went riding around. Had a blast! Drug Main two hours.

September 11
Mother is so damn mad at me she's about to have triplets and I sure don't know why! I think she's found out about Dale and me going to the "Wildcat" at noon, in fact I know that's what it is 'cause there's not another shittin' thing it COULD be. She took my phone out AGAIN & so HELL I know it's pretty bad. That old Fossil, I could kill her or better, make her wish she was dead. Dale called, FOSSIL answered! We talked a little while. Then that OLD BAG made me get off the phone. She'll remember that.

Thursday
At the mountains with Paula. My bathing suit top fell off in the river. EMBARRASSING! Got 2 letters from Susan. She said Dale is DRINKING and he stole some batteries and a motor and got put in JAIL! I don't know what's wrong with him. I just wish I was there with him. I'm going home tomorrow.

Saturday
Mother and Daddy won't speak to me, but I don't care. Somebody just called and Daddy answered

and said I couldn't talk 'cause I was studying. BULL!
Mother TOLD him to say that and if it was Dale I'll
never forgive her.

Sunday

Dale called me tonight. Oh, it was great to hear his
voice. He told me all about jail, it was AWFUL!!! I
love him sooo much!!! He asked me if I'd MARRY him
and he's not kidding. He said, "We'll have a beautiful
wedding and a beautiful marriage and a little girl that
looks just like you." Dale says we'll get married either
after school's out or after I graduate.

November 21

We broke up this morning. I went out to the car
and he talked and I sat. He said he wasn't true and
it wasn't fair for me. Oh God I wish I was dead! He
said he still loved me but he hadn't been true to me.
It wasn't fair to have me tied down and him not. He
asked me if I wanted to break up for a while and I
NODDED. He said he wouldn't be true, especially this
next week and I don't know what that means. I wish
it could of worked. I WAS so happy.

ADULT ME SAYS:

A couple of days after Dale and I broke up, I found out he'd
started dating his ex-girlfriend again.

Tuesday

I HATE DALE. I COULD make myself believe Dale only broke up with me because it wasn't fair for me but I don't. I just got shit on again and I'm sick of it. K-L-E-A played "I'm So Lonesome I Could Cry" . . . I did.

Thursday

I found out that she does have a little more ambition than to sit on her butt all day—SHE goes to B E A U T Y School! HA! Today at noon, they parked right in front of us. Boy! I 'bout blew my shittin' stack. Oh, he makes me sick! She had that ignorant scarf tied around her Pin Head and stuffing that food in her Pig Face with both of her hoofs! I looked over there and Dale was looking at us and I raised my eyebrows like "Boy, Mister, you're really tying one on!" I came home for the rest of the afternoon 'cause I was sick.

November 26

Paula called, said Dale told her he was getting married. I love Dale so much, God only knows how much, and knowing that breaks my heart all over again. Well, I've gotta get someone else whether I like it or not. That's all she wrote Dear John!

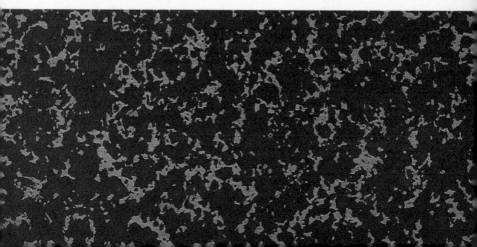

THE NEW GIRL

Leonard Hyman

Least Likely to . . . Be Quarterback

Growing up in American Samoa, I was the smartest kid in my school. My parents had moved there as Baha'i missionaries, and education was important to them. So I became a star student. Along with my best friend, Josh, I enjoyed life at the head of the class.

But the summer before seventh grade, Josh moved away. Suddenly, I was alone.

And that's when *she* arrived on campus.

Her name was Mele, and I have no idea where she came from or how or why. All I knew was that she bested me in every regard—she was instantly popular, devastatingly cute, and worst of all totally brilliant.

With my status as resident child genius threatened, I began to follow the wisdom of ancient philosophers: Keep your allies close but your enemies closer. Unfortunately, I took that to heart.

August 30

I love the 7th grade. I'm helping with the school newspaper, friends with the class and enjoying life! Weird! Wow! I just realized I never mentioned the geography bee! I won it! Anyway, back to the point. The newspaper is great! And the media instructor is cool!

September 5

I think Mele Parker is a witch. A WITCH!! So does
Misa, Solip, Hes, Olita, and a few other people. So we
are trying to come up with ways to make her feel bad.
Any way, I just found out she likes me, I mean loves
me. She's a witch. Here's the problem. Misa & Solip
have this plan that I'll like her and then dump her.
But what if this backfires? What if she kisses me or
asks me out (despite boys are supposed to ask girls.)
My life will be ruined! My first date/kiss will be with a
witch! Oh well, maybe I'll read up on insults to blow
off losers!

September 6

Finks! Misa and Solip are buttholes! They lied about
Mele liking me and today they told Sani who told
Mele that I like her! That is according to them. They
lie so much. I don't know what to believe. I may be
worrying about nothing. Maybe Mele doesn't have
a crush on me and Misa never told Sani. But, what
if they did tell Sani who told Mele. This is terrible if
Mele likes me and if she doesn't! Why me? The scary
part is the fact that everything is unknown.

Brilliant idea: The thing we should fear most is
the danger of the unknown.

Life sucks. Mele is getting popular. I think Mele
really does like me and I pray she does so I can
embarrass her and Misa and Solip instead of visa-
versa. I hope tomorrow never comes.

Today I started daydreaming about the problem

and Ms. Willis said I was spacing out and Olita
said I was daydreaming about my girlfriend. Mele's
head jerked up. Does she know something, or is she
hoping I do, or don't? Then Ms. Willis told us to talk
about personal affairs outside of class. I said "Yeah!"
Smooth move. Then they teased and said that I really
had a girlfriend.

I am weird.
Everything is weird.
Except my life . . .
It sucks.

September 7

The world hates me. The Misa, Solip, Mele incident
is over and Mele hates me. And most of the class
does, too. In the words of Bill Nye the science guy,
"consider the following." Maybe I should runaway. I
wish I didn't have a conscience. Then I'd . . . do a lot
of things.

October 14

What if my life ends up like my childhood, a total
zip? I need a friend or a girl or both. I'm lovesick.
I'm falling in love with every girl I see and expecting
love in return. Would you believe I even liked Mele
for about a half an hour? I should be out having fun,
instead I'm here explaining my thoughts to myself.
I'm a kid for gosh sakes. I NEED A LIFE! I'm young
and restless.

October 22

Dear Diary,

I've fallen in love with . . . Mele. Yes, the same Mele I called a witch. Now that I've become a better person, I've seen her good side and oooh! She's cute, funny, smart, talented, and beautiful. What a bod OOOH-WEEEE! I love her, more than I loved Sala. I now realize that Sala was toying with me. But now I love Mele. The soap opera continues . . . I think I may have a chance with her but I've thought that with all of my crushes with the same amount of conviction. Oh well, I love Mele Parker.

November 15

"Absence makes the heart grow fonder."

I'm speaking of Josh & Mele. I've only been gone from her a day, but I love her. She is just so missable. Josh, oohh, now Josh, I could, mmmph, him one or two. He's off having a life, with a girl. Well, that's according to the Ouija board. But if he is, man! He's having a life while I'm in the armpit of the universe! I'm going nuts! This whole I love Mele and don't have Josh have totally ruined my whole #@* life! I love her. She may/may not love me. Oh, by the way, there's going to be a new girl in our class on Monday. For some reason, I'm really excited. It may be my love for people, I don't know. Life's going to lead me to a disappointment, I know it. Oh well. I'm so joyful & happy. Let's not ruin it.

January 8

Well I was right, I was disappointed about the new
student. Liz, the new girl, has now joined Sara's "I'm
uncool" club! One mistake can ruin your life, and Liz
has made that mistake. I think she likes me (but then
in my mind everyone does.) She kept staring at me
during song practice. Oh well, I don't like her. She's
creepy. Oh, by the way yesterday Mele put her arms
around my neck to reach the keyboard. Her chest was
very close. Oooh-wee! It's hot!

January 16

Liz likes me still. Jun Wong thinks so too. He's not a
very reliable source, but still. I'm trying to be friends
with her at least but they still think I like her. She
keeps coming up to me and saying little things like,
"The zipper on your bag is open." Or some other little
remark. She always seems to be looking at me too.
Oh, well.

January 17

I'm starting to like Liz, as a friend mind you, nothing
more. I think that's the way she likes me, as a friend.
I'm just afraid I may start to *like* her, which could ruin
everything. I feel strange . . . as if nothing matters, life
goes on, life seems so pointless. What if I end up a
squat? I feel alone . . . alone.

January 18

Despite what it sounds like, I still love Mele. We were

teasing each other and we both really kept our cool even though I wrote on the computer, "Mele Parker is a lesbian prostitute who is having an affair with Madonna." She wrote something about me going to a surgeon and getting my dick cut off. Well, well, well. Aren't we sane? I love her, though.

She says she'll get me on Monday. I hope she does. I just wish something would happen in my life, you know? Something new. A date, a friend, something! My life just seems so . . . pointless!

February 17

Dear Diary,

My life sucks! However on the lighter side of my life, uh, uh, er, um, well, hmmmmmmm.

Well there is one thing kind of. Liz. According to Sara and my intuition, she likes me. I also like her. The thing is, I'm 11 she's 12. It would never work. She's different though. She isn't as pretty as Mele and not as mean or annoying as Sala. She's smarter, less girlie, and I love her.

Life is like a Rubik's Cube. It has so many sides, so many shades, and seems impossible.

O I'M NOT DROWNING. I really DO YOU SO THAT
. I Think you Think I'm hanging FROM THE R.J.
ee still but I'm NOT. I really enjoyed Getting TO
ow you These past two MONTHS, BUT I DON'
k your IN The Bend, and I'm Going out on The
b by saying That I The reason I DION'T Th
o were like I Thought I meant That I
Tst you were JUST DIFFERENT Than what I
excepted because I DION'T YOU
me ask you out with
want I you.

WELL THAT'S KIM
I UNDERSTAND. (I THINK)
THE PIKES PLAYING BASKET
why I Confuse you? Okay
mb and said, NO I
Above paragraph. That I

SPEECHLESS

Jennifer Anthony

Biggest Smart-Ass

THE F-WORD.

I DID THAT because I DIDN'T WANT YOU TO Think I
WAS WEIRD AND ThAT I WANTED TO ask you OUT. I DIDNT
Think YOU WOULD be INTERESTED in Going OUT WITH me SO
I JUST KIND OF looked The other way until ThAT MONDAY
Night on my way Home I said I was Going TO
ask Jennifer out! That's why I DID All That.

PRESENTS, I HAD FUN WHEN YOU CAME BECAUSE
WERE SO EASY TO TALK TO Jennifer KEPT STARING

When I was eighteen, I started dating a boy named Levi, an athletic and popular guy I'd had my eye on ever since his older brother had coached my basketball team. On our second date we found ourselves in his bedroom, lying side by side on his bed.

We were all alone in the house. We could have had sex, made out, or even just talked. But we were too nervous for any of that. So instead we sat inches apart, pulled out a blank notebook of binder paper . . . and wrote.

LEVI'S NOTE:
I came home last night after our date and fell asleep.
What did you do, besides think about me?

JENNIFER'S NOTE:
I did sit-ups, and leglifts, and talked to Sharry on
the phone about our date. Sharry thinks you're a
gentleman.

LEVI'S NOTE:
Well, that's nice. I was a gentleman and I didn't throw
myself all over you like a wet blanket. That's one of
my rules.

JENNIFER'S NOTE:
What are your *other* rules for dating?

LEVI'S NOTE:
What do you *want* my other rules to be? I was surprised when you said yes to go out with me. Tony asked me if I had fun with you and I said yes, and I think you're really cool.

JENNIFER'S NOTE:
I told Sharry that I had a very fun time with you. She said she was jealous, and I told her I was looking forward to today. What else did Tony say?

LEVI'S NOTE:
He said, "Don't jump in with both feet! Ha ha ha ha ha ha! You like her, don't you?" He just giggled and said "Ha ha ha ha ha." I want to take you out again sometime. I would have to ask you out again. I like talking to you. You're very interesting. I like that. I don't think, I know, therefore I speak.

JENNIFER'S NOTE:
That was *very* philosophical. You are fun to talk with on the phone. Stephanie can't believe how long we talked! I really am tempted to tickle you right now.

LEVI'S NOTE:
That would not be a good move. I would tickle you back. I really want to stress that I would like to take

you out again. Will you go? Anyway, I dove in and now I am drowning! Cool, huh?

JENNIFER'S NOTE:
Yes, definitely. Or does that sound too eager? Maybe I should say, "Let me check my calendar." Do you really think you're drowning?

LEVI'S NOTE:
No, I'm not drowning. I really do _____ you so that's that. I really enjoyed getting to know you these past two months. I'm going out on the limb by saying that the reason I didn't think you were like I thought meant that I thought you were just different than what I expected because I didn't think you would just let me ask you out without ground rules. I just meant I _____ you.

JENNIFER'S NOTE:
Well, *that's* kind of vague. But I think I understand. (I think.) But when I saw you playing basketball, you confused me.

LEVI'S NOTE:
Why did I confuse you? Okay, I went out on a limb and said . . . No! I told you in the above paragraph that I like you, dammit! Is that still vague?

JENNIFER'S NOTE:
I totally thought we were just the f-word.

I was such a total prude that even "the f-word" referred to being friends.

LEVI'S NOTE:
Well I'm glad I asked you out. I hate that f-word.
What veggies do you like? I thought I would be a
pervert to ask someone in high school out when I was
in college. I wanted to shake your hand last night but
I didn't. I was going to kiss your hand good night.

JENNIFER'S NOTE:
You wanted to shake my hand? That would be
awkward. Steph said you were like Tony because
you're so nice, not like most other guys.

LEVI'S NOTE:
I hope I can keep taking you out if you let me. I think
you're really neat!

JENNIFER'S NOTE:
Let's make up some rules for dating.

At this point, Levi and I took turns writing our rules for dating in the notebook.

JENNIFER'S NOTE:
Rule #1—Never talk back on the first date.

LEVI'S NOTE:
Rule #2—Never run out of gas.

JENNIFER'S NOTE:
Rule #3—Never get physical on the first date
(includes kissing, shaking hands).

LEVI'S NOTE:
Rule #4—Learn her name.

JENNIFER'S NOTE:
Rule #5—Make sure that you don't have Gloria
Estefan tapes in your car.

LEVI'S NOTE:
Rule #6—Always carry a stopwatch.

JENNIFER'S NOTE:
Rule #7—Never put your arm around your date in
the movies.

LEVI'S NOTE:
Rule #8—Always go to a Chinese restaurant with
more than one waiter.

JENNIFER'S NOTE:
Rule #9—No f-word before the date.

LEVI'S NOTE:
Rule #10—Never jump in with your feet first—always jump in with your head first.

JENNIFER'S NOTE:
Rule #11—Never fart, burp, or vomit on the first date.

LEVI'S NOTE:
Rule #12—Even though you're tempted, thou shall not break any rules.

LEVI'S NOTE:
To end this series of talk notes. I just wanted to say that I really have fun when I'm with you and rule #3 (don't get physical) was the one I almost broke. But you looked so nice last night, and I really wanted to kiss you. But I'm glad I did not because patience is a virtue.

JENNIFER'S NOTE:
I can't believe how much fun I've had today and all we've done is sit, eat, write notes, and eat more. I wanted to kiss you too but I wasn't going to jump over into the driver seat and do it.

LEVI'S NOTE:
Why didn't you do that?

JENNIFER'S NOTE:
Yeah, right! Why did you go out with that girl for three months and not kiss her? Just wondering.

LEVI'S NOTE:
Because I chose not to.

JENNIFER'S NOTE:
Guys are pretty unpredictable. You never know if they're telling the truth.

LEVI'S NOTE:
I'm not lying to you! I DO LIKE YOU! Okay, I'll tone it down a bit. I mean that's what I've been trying to tell you, why you're not like I expected. I like the way you are and the way you have a great sense of humor and that's not all.

JENNIFER'S NOTE:
I feel the same way. I feel weird saying it because I don't usually after going out with a guy once.

LEVI'S NOTE:
Oh well! That's nice! So that's all she wrote! But you never answered my question—can I keep taking you out?

JENNIFER'S NOTE:
Yes. I would really like to keep going out with you.

lationship " is no longer in my vocabulary
d i am a disposable whore - I am not close
~~[scribbled out]~~

n having fun, thats all that matters right
can be quoted saying while i kis
son and plan to get down their fr
nts.
Self respect is wh
d if you do try not
Ya can look in th
e Sample ... Free
m I !
~~[scribbled out]~~

MCC
Angry Erotica
Least Likely to . . . Win an Arm Wrestle

it. I can't hear what you say, i
e ya with your eyes rolling into the
yours head, depositing your poison

On my knees once again ...

Being Poisoned is better than being

For those of you who haven't grown up gay and Catholic, I highly suggest it. It's a real pleasure. I fought it for a long time. I prayed constantly. "Dear God, please have Mattel make a Madeline Kahn fashion doll I can have and hold and call my own. And please make me straight as well."

It seemed to work for a while. I developed massive crushes on girls with very Irish names. I would give them very sensual hugs and snap bracelets. All was well. My prayers had been answered.

It wasn't until I learned how to "pleasure myself" (slapping and/or rubbing my boy parts against anything stationary) that I realized there was a problem. A big problem. Visions of Irish boys danced in my head. And Italian boys. And occasionally a Polish boy.

In order to rectify the situation, I would try to pleasure myself using images of females. I had this big collage of Tori Spelling pictures on my wall. To me, she was the image of beauty, what with that long face and those dark roots. I'd stand there, in front of my well-laid-out collage, and try to work it up. Donna Martin graduates. Donna Martin graduates. Donna Martin graduates. Not even a drip.

When that didn't work, I tried Anna Nicole Smith.

When that didn't work, I knew I was gay.

So I embraced it. I had no choice. When I got to high

119

school, I hooked up with "curious" straight men and subsequently fell in love with them. When they didn't love me back, I did what any self-respecting crazy honors student would do to regain his dignity. I wrote angry erotic poems.

HARLOT 3/29/95

A Male Lilith is what I am . . .
Craving your nocturnal emissions . . .
Don't care if emotion is attached
Just let your demon spawn crawl down my throat and
rip apart my insides
A sweet and salty potion that turns my eyes red
And gives me heart burn.
Screw Nocturnal!
Emit the juices morning, noon and night.
I will be here waiting for every last drop.
I'm swallowing your sweet battery acid shake . . .
RATTLE & ROLL on the cold cement floor.
Who ever said a man can't be a harlot witch and
whore?
Proven wrong once again.
I am thirsty . . .
Thirsty for abuse.

SUMMER POISON (1995)

Wholesome, pure, worked from emotion.
Smiled and brought you out of that shell.
Best friends together, yet you alone sent me to HELL.
Alone in your room, parents asleep.

YOU smiled and offered YOUR pleasure to me . . .

It seemed rather churlish to decline.

"Hey. I'm up for it."

Hand on thigh. Rubbing stomach. Moan & wimper.

Nose running, tears streaming, gag reflex just barely there.

Back & forth, back & forth.

Break that neck boy. I hope you like it.

Poison released. Purpose served.

Old sleeping bag, cold floor, pulverated heart.

Thank YOU!

Repeat process.

"It's all about experimentation. What are feelings?

You are a disposable tongue and mouth."

Vomit—Purge myself of your poison which has changed me forever.

Wholesome and pure no more!

I smile still, but in a tainted way.

I say my line with a smirk and one eyebrow raised.

I'm better when I think of you . . . emotions are just a joke.

I'm sweet when I'm on my knees trying to flush out your poison with theirs.

"RELATIONSHIP" is no longer in my vocabulary.

And I am a disposable whore . . . close to no one but myself.

Self respect is what you make of it . . .

And if you try not to think about it, you can look in the mirror in the morning.

FREE SAMPLE FREE SAMPLE FREE SAMPLE AM I!

I look into your eyes, but don't be fooled.
I'm not deep. I'm not trying to connect with your
heart.
I can't hear what you say.
I just see you with your eyes rolling into the back of
your head.
Depositing your poison.

On my knees once again.
Being poisoned is better than being alone.

HEAD GAMES

Kate Augustine

Least Likely to . . . Stay in Ohio

I grew up in rural Ohio. To give you an idea of just how country it was, my high school was in the middle of a fifty-acre cornfield. Every year we had Tractor Day—when kids drove their tractors to school. As you might imagine, there wasn't much to do out there, and I wanted out. So when I got to high school, I devised a three-part fail-safe plan to pave my road to freedom:

1. Brains. I became a straight-A student and horrendous teacher's pet.

2. Boys. I started dating Mr. Right (since replaced) when I was a freshman.

3. Fashion. I tight-rolled my jeans and sported the bang claw.

As a result, I became known as a go-to girl for any kind of guidance. Acne. Arguments. Intercourse. Helping others helped me feel less trapped and more worldly.

So when a girlfriend asked me for some advice about her boyfriend junior year, I dutifully wrote her this helpful letter to explain the "ins and outs" of eleventh-grade dating.

Hi! ☺
Okay, here we go . . .

125

Before you "go down"—kiss his niples, kinda run your tongue around it, then suck on it and stuff.

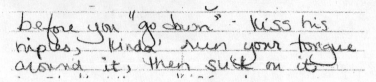

Then, kiss down his stomach. You'll have to use your hand, too—to hold it. Start by runnin' your tongue on the end. (It should make him get excited—& stuff.) Make sure you have your lips nice and wet—and bend them over your teeth. Put a little of "IT" in your mouth.

Maybe run your tongue around on it. Work your way up to it. Don't try to put it all in your mouth at once. Kinda in and out, in and out, until you can. And you don't have to put it ALL in. So use your hand (well, fingers), to rub the bottom up and down with how you're moving.

It's neat, though. It's really soft and smooth. BUT, I've never had him "lose it" in my mouth. He almost has, but you can kinda tell when they're gonna. It'll like, move weird. Also, like take breaks—in and out—lick and stuff—keep licking your lips—kiss his thighs or abdomen or stomach or nipples.

There's a few other "options"—I'll just tell you though! ☺

Well, got any questions—go ahead and ask! ☺ (Anything!! ☺)

"Heart" Ya, (Me)

PS—I found out there really isn't a "wrong" way, unless you use your teeth!

PPS—A LITTLE teeth are OK. Like if you're REAL gentle and run your teeth on like the "head". But only for a second. Kinda "daring." He may or may not like that.

Don't feel bad if you slip and a little teeth are used. Just kiss it and make it all better! ☺

FAST FOOD ROMANCE

Erin Carter

Least Likely to . . . Talk

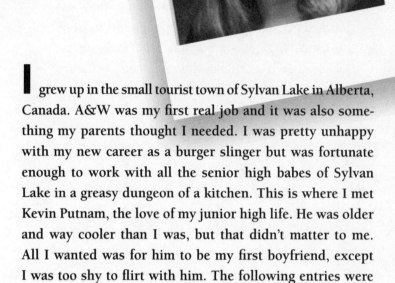

I grew up in the small tourist town of Sylvan Lake in Alberta, Canada. A&W was my first real job and it was also something my parents thought I needed. I was pretty unhappy with my new career as a burger slinger but was fortunate enough to work with all the senior high babes of Sylvan Lake in a greasy dungeon of a kitchen. This is where I met Kevin Putnam, the love of my junior high life. He was older and way cooler than I was, but that didn't matter to me. All I wanted was for him to be my first boyfriend, except I was too shy to flirt with him. The following entries were written in the summer after grade nine and the beginning of grade ten.

August 10, 1995

I had the wickedest dream last night. Kevin was in it. Actually so were Nicky, Danny James and Rob. Most of these guys are from A&W.

In my dream we're all working in A&W, but the kitchen was like a big dungeon. At first, it started to be just normal A&W but then it grew into a huge giant kitchen, everything was bigger than it was supposed to be.

Anyways I woke up after the best part. It was when Kevin and I were standing at the counters. I think we were doing onion rings. He put his hand on my shoulder. I looked up and smiled. He smiled back. Then he moved his hand down my arm and touched my hand. I took the opportunity. I squeezed his hand. He gave me a big smile. My face lit up. We looked at each other for awhile and then I woke up. Awesome dream hey?

I swear that when I was dreaming that my heart was just about banging out of my chest. I have no idea if we'll ever get together, but at least I know the guy this time. I have a feeling we might though. I just love him (you know what I mean?). He is the kind of guy I've been looking for; Funny, a good personality. Plus I think I'm in his science class. Wicked hey!!

I think that I'm psychic. Once I dreamt that I had my period and the next day I had it. Also once in A&W I was thinking about what this guy was going to order and I thought "teen burger and a large fry." I was right. Maybe the dream that I just had about Kevin will come true. Just maybe.

All my A&W buddies are off on vacation except Danny Boy. But I only work an hour and a half with him this week. Bummer. Nicky went to basketball camp this week, and next week I'm going to Grandma and Grandpa's. Kevin went to Vancouver for two weeks. Now I'm bummed out. Two whole weeks without seeing my buddies, how will I make it?

School starts in two weeks. Right on. This summer was the best. I got my learners permit and everything.

Nicky is my favourite guy friend right now. He always complains to me that we never get the same shifts anymore. He always gets mad when I leave work before him. (You gotta love him.) Danny asked about my Arabic necklace. I told him where I got it and that I lived there. He asked a lot of questions and then he started teasing me. Gotta love him too.

September 23, 1995

Really important news flash. I was in the freezer at A&W looking for the chicken chunks and they were way at the top shelf. As I was pulling the box, a big bag of chicken chunks fell all over the floor. The next thing I knew Kevin was back by the freezer looking in (I was down on the floor picking up chicken chunks). He started laughing. All I could say was oops.

QUESTION: Did he come running back there because he heard the crash and wanted to see if I was all right? Or did Marlo send him back there? I dunno. I hope it was the first one. What am I going to write on the back of my picture to him?

Hey Kevin,
Come back to A&W. It's not the same without you.
Erin Carter
AKA Wembley
Is that too forward?
Or
Hey Kevin
A&W is not the same since you left . . .

This is what I wrote on the back of Nicky's picture:

Hey Nicky

You and Danny are the best people to work with at A&W. Kevin too except he quit.

Erin AKA Wembley

Or

Kevin

Next summer you better apply at A&W or I quit

Just kidding

Erin

Or

I'm going on strike. No more English for the rest of the year! Do you agree with me?

Erin AKA Wembley

This is what I actually put.

Kevin

Your plan has worked. All my friends insist on calling me Wembley.

Well have a good year.

Erin

(Don't expect me to sign as Wembley)

Just kidding.

Tomorrow I'm going to give Kevin my picture in English class. I'm so nervous. Today Tracey told Jesse that she liked him. Guess what, he liked her. Don and Shannon are practically going out and Serge likes Pam. Poor Erin.

My pictures turned out pretty good. Tracey says that mine are the best out of all of ours. As if.

I want to go out with Kevin! Why can't he be psychic? Tomorrow when I give him my picture I'm going to tell him that he owes me a picture now. And if he doesn't have any left, then he has to draw his picture perfectly.

And I won't say just kidding.

MALE CHAUVINIST GEEK

GJ Echternkamp

Most Likely to . . . Photocopy and Compile
All Printed Articles on the Video Game
Street Fighter II in a Large Binder and
Call It the Echternkamp Bible

When I was fourteen, I tested out of junior high and went straight from the eighth grade to college. I imagine if you look in the dictionary under "nerd," you might see my student ID. My nicknames as a kid were actually Poindexter and Doogie.

By the age of fifteen I realized I'd rather be seen as cool. So I had a makeover. I bought contact lenses, grew my hair out, and stopped wearing shirts with my name monogrammed on the pocket. And suddenly I got attention from girls. This was nothing less than a revelation, so I started keeping a computer journal of my "exploits." I wrote with such confidence and cynicism. But in reality I was still a nerd, and I didn't have the confidence to even *hug* a girl, let alone hold her hand.

Despite what you are about to read—I'm really quite likable, I swear.

February 10

Well, it's been a while since I've written. It's February 10, 1994. Today, I realized something horrible. I just discovered a new form of depression: the infectious nature of being a teenager. I AM NOW GIRL CRAZY. It all began with a waitress. Her name is Chris and she has perfect lips. PERFECT. Naturally, I started fantasizing about what it would be like to kiss Chris. And then I thought of her giving me a blow-job.

What has happened to me? From being overly happy last week, I feel so empty, so alone. I ran into a bunch of the popular crowd at McDonalds. Oh, how I long to be amongst their simplicity. They fuck around, do nothing important, yet have fun. They do teenage things, like go to clubs. They're so dumb, yet I long to be of that life again.

April 15

I spent a lot of time with Jody over the holidays. The hunt has been won, so I feel it is time to abandon the carcass. I feel very, very empty. The pleasure that Jody gave me is gone. I want the chase. I've been trying to get Elizabeth.

I'm so sick of the same pretty face, the same nice ass, the same cool personality. I don't care what I get, I just want something new. Something . . . virgin. I want a virgin. I WANT ELIZABETH. I feel so empty. I want to talk to Elizabeth on the phone. I want to act in a play. I want to paint my little figures. I want to ACCOMPLISH SOMETHING. I want to fuck Jenny, as well, to spread her skinny legs. To see her bent over as I fuck her from behind. TO BREAK A HYMEN . . . ah the thrills that will never await me. I wish I could release all this tension, and just spank the inchworm.

May 19

Even more time has passed. It is May 19 of 1994.

Jody, whom I was going to leave, cut me to the quick. She wanted to break up, but still stay in contact. She wanted a middle path. I was fucking shocked. Who would have guessed that the bitch, who I carried on my shoulders for so long, would want to break up! It's so unlike the caring, loving bitch I thought she was. Don't get the wrong idea, I don't wish anything bad upon her . . . I just have a somewhat pleasurable feeling knowing that she tormented, and therefore lost, the best fucking guy in the world. She'll end up with tons of kids, and never amount to a hill of vibrating pens. I, on the other hand, intend to succeed.

Well, thus begins a new chapter in my life.

Jody is dead, long live Elizabeth!

May 23

It's Monday . . . I talked to Elizabeth . . . and well . . . Shit, man, she fuckin' loves me . . .I got me so many brownie points I'll never spend em all.

May 28

It's now Saturday, and I realize my affliction. I have a case of "Girl-of-the-Day Syndrome." Everyday, I am obsessed with a new woman. Yesterday, Jody was on my mind. Today, it was Chris. I learned today that Chris is GORGEOUS. She is fucking adorable. Her ass is the classic upside-down heart. I wish my dick could make it a spade. Anywho, back to the girl crazy thing. I like Elizabeth . . . I do! I just want them *all*. I've never been like this before. When I considered myself a "Brain" I just assumed that women didn't find me attractive, so I didn't care, nor didn't try. But now I'm popular. All of a sudden, girls love me. I've got them flirting with me everywhere!

GOD! I'm depressing myself. I better find a new hobby.

June 1

The human body, when properly looked at, is a splendid thing. A beauty to all the senses. There is one part of the body that is not so pleasant . . . sometimes, it borders repulsive. This, of course, is the genitals. It really isn't fair. It's like God made this smooth, perfect, flowing creature, and he named it woman. Then he spread her silken legs, took a harpoon, and rammed into her repeatedly. Not a nice little slit, to match the rest of her sleekness, no, a lipped, hairy thing that excretes liquids. And God, in his infinite wisdom, gave it an odor, and every man an intense desire to put part of his body inside this sloppy, floppy chasm.

Don't get me wrong. The male's genitals aren't so pleasant, either. A sagging, furry scrotum is certainly not pleasant. It's a shame that behind every beautiful girl and perfect body lies, hidden in between legs, under clothes, a lurker. The lurker is there, in all it's shaggy, wrinkled, smelly glory. And it waits . . . with every step it rubs its lips together in anticipation. I want it, but I don't like it. Well, there go my hymen-breaking dreams.

June 4

I went to a play with Elizabeth last night, and I think it's love. I really do. But there is a disadvantage with affection, the further you go, the less thrilling the minor stuff becomes.

How do I begin to explain the cataclysmic changes going on? Not in the usual sense, oh no. Not puberty, just a social life. And my schoolwork is suffering. Really suffering.

I flirt with every single girl who is slightly decent.

Here's the deal. I am just not satisfied anymore. If I can get the classic ass type A, I also want ass type B, and ass type C, and just about every somewhat good looking shape of derriere there has ever been. When I have a blond, I also want a brunette. It's not that the grass is greener on the other side, I just want both sides. I like Elizabeth a lot, but my hormones want more. My hormones could push me to commit thought crimes against her. Thought crimes that may become reality crimes.

I think my dream screw would be Uma Thurman as Venus from *Baron Munchausen*.

July 2

I haven't written here in a while, so I guess I'll fill in the two biggest factors in my life.

Lyle Lovett. The Ascension to Sex.

Basically, I'm really into Lyle, and I'm getting closer to breaking the big H. So far, I made it to third base (with clothing barrier), given her multiple orgasms in various ways, and touched bare breast. My goal is approaching extremely quickly. So far, Mr. Willy hasn't been touched yet, but I figure that'll happen after the hymen is broken.

July 10

I am in love with Elizabeth. I know it now. I had an extremely long talk with her . . . and explained to her many different aspects of my life. My concept of time . . . of love . . . of death . . . of religion . . . my past . . . my relationship with her . . . my ego . . . It was my entire life of brooding, judging, deliberating . . . all in one conversation. And she understood. She understood me. I'm going to marry the fuck out of her . . .

And so I leave this chapter with this . . .

Garp taught me a lesson . . . affairs are tragedies

Excalibur taught me, as well . . .

Lust can, and will, destroy Empires

But most importantly, *The Princess Bride* taught me this

TRUE LOVE EXISTS.

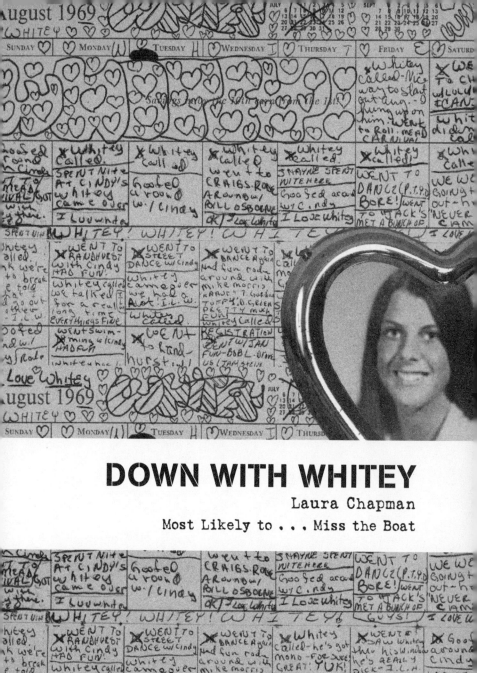

DOWN WITH WHITEY

Laura Chapman

Most Likely to . . . Miss the Boat

I entered high school in Palatine, Illinois, during the late 1960s. There was a lot going on in the world then. Civil rights. Vietnam. None of which seemingly entered my world. Indeed, while radicals a mere thirty miles away in Chicago held protests, screaming "Down with Whitey," I quietly battled my own version.

His nickname was Whitey, for his light-blond hair and pale skin, and I hated that I loved him. If I couldn't be with him . . . I wanted to be over him. My obsession with Whitey began during the end of my freshman year in 1969 and lasted for my entire sophomore, junior, and senior years. I was finally liberated from him—appropriately enough—on the Fourth of July in 1972.

After two agonizing months of growing infatuation (on my part), we started dating after listening to a band at the New Place. While the band played Janis Joplin, I flirted with Whitey by singing along to the music: "Come on, come on . . . take another piece of my heart now, baby." I had no idea that he would take me literally.

I should also point out that instead of a journal or diary, I recorded everything in four mini calendars.

1969
Mar 28 Started to like Whitey.

Apr 15   I really like Whitey but he'd never like me.

May 12   I have a mad crush on Whitey.

May 21   I have a horrible crush on Whitey. I. L. W.

ADULT ME SAYS:

Otherwise known as "I Love Whitey."

May 30   Went to New Place. Rode home with Whitey.

ADULT ME SAYS:

For the next three months, Whitey's name appears in my calendar 139 times along with 148 hearts.

Aug 10   Whitey called. I think we're going to break up! He told me that I should go out with other guys. I. L. W.

Aug 11   Whitey called. We talked for a real long time. EVERYTHING'S FINE.

Aug 14   Whitey called. He's got mono! GREAT! YUK!

Aug 15   Went and saw Whitey thru his window. He's really sick.

Aug 22   Went to see Whitey—he's pure white!

Aug 27   I hate Whitey. He hasn't called for six days.

Sept 8   Whitey called. Our conversations are getting really boring. I bet he hates me!

Sept 14   Whitey called. Our conversations are getting tons better!

Sept 26   Whitey and I broke up. I. L. W.

Sept 28   Whitey's gonna call me on TUESDAY.

Sept 30   Whitey called me tonite—we're <u>good</u> friends.

BIG DEAL!

Oct 10   Went to party at Steve's. Made out with
Whitey. He said he missed me. I LOVE Whitey!
Oct 12   Don called. Found out that Whitey was just
using me. I HATE WHITEY!!!
Nov 24   Whitey smiled at me. Big SHIT!
Dec 1   I hope this month turns out better than last
one did! My goal is to get Whitey!

1970

Jan 11   Whitey called. I think he hates me—I don't
know why—but I think so.
Jan 24   Whitey was gonna come over but he didn't.
He went over to Melissa's and Mara's—but he didn't
come here. Something better change pretty soon or
I'm gonna break up with him. We're supposed to go
out tomorrow, but I know we won't.
Jan 30   I'm going out with Don tomorrow.
Feb 1   Don told Victor that he had fun last night—
good! Because maybe he told Whitey and he'll ask me
out!
Feb 2   I can't think about anything except Whitey.
Feb 5   Don called. We're going out on Saturday. I
wish I was going out with Whitey, but I can always
close my eyes and pretend.
Feb 21   Went to the show with Don. Saw *Easy Rider*.
I was really starting to like him, then we went to
Jack-in-the-Box and Whitey drove by. Five minutes
later he pulled in right next to us. I saw him. I
stopped liking Don right then.

Mar 13   Whitey came over. Had a riot. He hates me.

Mar 15   Whitey was goofing around with Kim. I can tell he likes her. I hate Kim.

Mar 18   YUK! Whitey & Don called. Friday night I'm going out with Don, and we're going to double with Kim and Whitey! Yuk! That's going to be horrible!!

Mar 20   Don, Whitey, Kim and I went to see *Bob & Carole & Ted & Alice*. It was really good.

ADULT ME SAYS:

And this had to be Whitey's idea.

Mar 28 Went to confession with Cindy. That was fun.

Mar 31   I wish we'd move so that I could forget about Whitey. I wonder if I would even then.

May 9   Went downtown to see *A Man Called Horse*. It was gross. Had fun.

Jun 13   Whitey came over. I can't believe he likes me. Maybe he doesn't!

Aug 20   Everything's going just great. Flunked Driver's Ed & Whitey still didn't call.

Sep 2   Whitey called. He told me he loved me. I love him so much.

Sep 5   WOW! Went to Jim's party. Yuk. Everything went KAPUT! No more Whitey.

Sep 22   Don called. I think I really like him.

Sep 24   Don called. I don't think I like him.

Sep 30   My face is the biggest ZIT! I know now why I don't have a boyfriend. SHIT!

Oct 16   Wonder what Whitey's been doing with

himself. Not that I really care or anything.

Oct 31   Went to party at O'Brien's. God. Whitey's not too big of a flirt. He treats Kim as bad as he treated me.

Nov 4   OH NO! Whitey called me and guess what? 3 guesses. I said I'd go out with him Saturday. Am I stupid or what! This is gonna be the last time I go out with him! I hope Don doesn't ask me out—cause I don't want anyone to know about this!

Nov 9   I know this shouldn't bother me at all, but I'm sad that Whitey didn't call me. Remember, Laura, you don't like him anymore—almost forgot.

Nov 11   Whitey came over. I guess I'm kinda back with him, but I told him I'm not gonna take half the shit I took from him before.

Nov 17   Whitey and I went to McDonald's. He really has changed. I love him.

Nov 22   Bought some Brut for Whitey.

Nov 30   Yay! November is over! This has been the best month of my life!

Dec 18   Called Whitey at 12:30. I'm never doing that again.

1971

Jan 23   Whitey called. He was gonna call back, but he didn't. I love him.

Jan 26   Whitey told me that he's writing to a girl who lives in Michigan—screw her!!!!!

Jan 30   Whitey called & we broke up. It was a mutual thing—so no hard feelings. Crap.

Jan 31   Well, this was my first full day of freedom and it sucks!

Feb 7   Whitey got a super ugly coat.

Feb 8   I hate weekends cause there's never anything to do but think about Whitey.

Feb 9   I just realized today that I'm glad Whitey and I broke up. But why in the hell won't he call me?

Feb 21   Whitey is a self-centered bastard! And I love him.

Mar 4   Wonder how Whitey's "pen-pal" is!

Apr 16   Whitey and Kim are back together.

Apr 20   I was right about Kim and Whitey. But I honestly don't care. I've finally realized that he's not what I made him up to be. Like what's he doing with his life—*Nothing*—he just doesn't have a future. I swear he'll never grow out of his have fun all the time stage.

Jul 19   Betsy thinks she has an ulcer. Good. Cindy's got mono and I have cancer of the vagina!

Jul 26   I really think I like Steve.

Jul 30   Went to the drive-in with Steve. He's going to call tomorrow. I'm finally over Whitey! Yay Rah!!

Aug 1   DAMN! I still love Whitey.

Aug 6   I'm so mixed up. I know I still love Whitey— but I can't. So I have to force myself to be with Steve.

Aug 7   Cindy & I went to Steve's. WHAT A NIGHT! I was with Whitey. What's my problem! He's only lying to me. I know it!

Aug 12   Whitey might have Scarlet Fever. Good!

Sept 25   Went to Hoffman's with Betsy. Whitey was yelling at me. This was it. This was the first time he's ever said he'd never even like me again.

Sept 27   I wonder if I'll ever be the same again.

Dec 20   Steve's having a New Year's Eve party. $5 to get in, tho. But I really want to go. Whitey will be there....

Dec 21   Talked to Whitey. He's trying so hard to change. I love him.

"Advanced Planning for 1972" NEVER GO BACK WITH WHITEY!

1972

Feb 8   I got Whitey a Valentine yesterday. He'll probably hate it.

Mar 5   Ouija board said I'd live with "W" in 1976!!!

Apr 8   Bob came over. He said Whitey couldn't come cause he was sick. Brother—Whitey must really think I'm dumb. I AM to like him!

Jul 3   Whitey called. Went to his house. He left to another party. I went there too. He was mad. I think it's goodbye Whitey.

July 4   Whitey went to Carl's. He had hickeys all over his neck. He didn't say one word to me all day.

ADULT ME SAYS:

When I got home that night, I carefully outlined the picture of the Liberty Bell—including the crack—and wrote my own Declaration of Independence.

July 4   FUCK WHITEY!

ESCAPE FROM PLANET TEXAS

Lacy Coil

Least Likely to . . . Borrow Your Madonna CD

In 1993 I was thirteen years old and living in a small town in North Central Texas. I had no boyfriend, no social life, no self-esteem, and on top of that my family life was in complete turmoil. In short, everything felt like a complete hopeless mess until Amy Erickson, from my third-period art class, gave me this: a poorly dubbed 180-minute mix tape of the Smiths.

Finally, I got a glimpse into a world beyond Denton, Texas. A world where being depressed, lonely, and celibate was poetic and glamorous. All I had to do ... was get there.

Whenever I feel overwhelmed and don't know what to do, I write out a plan. And in February of 1993 this was my plan: to get as far away from Denton as possible.

I never want to see anybody ever again. I want to be a hermit, I really do. What I need to do is:

A. Come into an immense sum of money.

B. Borrow it.

C. Put the money in a Swiss account.

D. Finish high school.

E. Take my easel, stereo, art supplies and Bear [my dog]

F. Ship them to Wales.

G. Buy an extensive piece of seaside property in rural Wales.

H. Buy a plane and learn to fly it.

I. Buy a car

J. Still have enough money for art supplies and utilities and food and notebooks.

K. Only be visited by Steven Morrissey, Kurt Vonnegut Jr., Anne Rice

L. Make these 3 people live as long as me and I'll never be lonely.

M. Live the rest of my life in ~~perfection~~ comfort and pleasure and friends.

~~THE END~~ not quite.

N. Have a total hysterectomy

O. Sell my art and writings until I pay back the money from letters A–C

P. Become the Morrissey of either art or literature

Q. Never run out of Swiss Mocha Decaffeinated Gourmet coffee with Irish Cream.

R. Not have any mirrors in my house

S. Have a Calvin Klein wardrobe

T. Have a bicycle

U. Be happy.

(sing this)

Break up the family!*,

And let's begin to live our lives!*

The End, but I hope not.

*By Morrissey, not me. I'm not that clever.

Since I knew I was taking my life into my own hands, I decided to set my affairs in order, which meant writing a letter to the boy I was completely in love with, who, to be fair, knew I was alive. He just didn't know much besides that.

I never want to see anybody ever again

Dear Tyler,
Hello, my darling. I must ask you to read this letter solemnly, and not to think me too melodramatic and fatalistic, etc. And so, I'll begin.

I am writing this on an airplane aimed towards London. I've got my art supplies and a toothbrush, and that's all I ever really wanted. There is an excellent chance I will die of starvation or exposure in England. I really don't care. However, I do want to tell you this: you WERE the only one I ever fell in love with. "See how words as old as sin fit me like a glove." (yes, Morrissey.) I'm sure my sappy little confession is merely a cliché to you, but with an idiotic hope it might not be, once more I am abandoning all pride.

Maybe I am wrong about you. Maybe you *are* only what you seem to be. Maybe I know more about you than you know or even want to know. I most certainly don't know. But I *am* something more. Maybe I just wanted you to see me as that all along. Anyhow, I love you. If I thought I was anything to you, I would give up everything for you as I am now. I would follow you anywhere and do anything just to see you. Trivial words and useless sentences, I know. But please remember me. I truly do love you—oh, Angel, angel, down we go together, in my mind at least. Let me keep that.

I love you.

ADULT ME SAYS:

Finally, I just *went* for it. It was time to live the dream.

Today I thought about going to London with all my art supplies, a pair of underwear, and a toothbrush. Cut off all my hair, and maybe just walk cross-country some fall or spring.
London is impractical because
a) It's too cold
b) I can't physically defend myself
c) I'm always sick
d) What would I do when I go on the rag?
The only good things about it would be:
a) People in Denton would idolize me.
b) London is REALLY neat.

I could sleep by the lions in Trafalgar Square, wake up early every morning, and wash my face in the fountain. Sure, it sounds like a dream. Find somewhere and say, "This is neat. I think I'll live here." Live on the Tower of London Green (!) or Picadilly Circus and form some sort of Palare. Maybe I could get a job—yeah! Work in a music store where I sell Moze paraphenelia. Hurrah man. Be very skinny from not eating and model. Sleep in the Victoria Gardens. Maybe I could be a mudlarker. O joy! Or hair wraps—I'd teach myself.

I could work in a bakery. Maybe if I were pretty enough, a real glamorous store would want me to bring in people. Maybe go on to Stratford and be a Royal Shakespeare Company stagehand, and then a ticket salesgirl, then an extra, an alternate, a character . . . then, the *lead actress* for the Royal Shakespeare Company! Five standing ovations on my off nights!

If I got tired of that, I could cross the English Channel and hike to Spain. I could do everything I did in England (except the music store) and tutor English for Spanish children, $5 per hour, guaranteed results.

Si usted no es satisfecho, no tendra que pagar. Le prometo.

Then, once I'd mastered Spanish, I'd have a trade there! Plus my drawings and meager acting talent. Then I'd go to another country—maybe Italy. Yeah, Italy. Italian'll be easy to pick up. I'll just have to keep in upper-class sections if I want to sound professional enough to tutor.

Then back to England—back to the old places— and on to Wales. Work on a fishing boat or as a worker on a sheep farm. I can clean, too. I could be a maid. Then to Ireland. Teach Italian and/or Spanish, baker, farm hand, sailor, artist, music seller, model if I'm good enough! Even a writer and actress! My memoirs will be priceless after such a life! Oh, God, this sounds so wonderful! I could do this, I think—yes, yes, I can! I can design, I can build, I can do it ALL—I could be a tour guide!

Well—maybe once I really knew England, Italy, Spain, France, Wales, and Ireland. I could take parties on tours—and I'd interview them to see if they'd be suitable "traveling companions." Oh, I could take them hitchhiking, the way I went! Keep up enough money for a little comfortable house in Killary Bay, have some big dogs, a cat or two—maybe even keep a husband there! Oh, God! Life holds so much! And I can have it—what I want! I can be a princess or a pauper or president—ANYTHING!

Oh, and then I'd come back to Denton, but I can never go back home. Haunt the backyard and shop and barn and meadow. "Here is where we trained the bird dogs. This is where we fished. This was the compost pile. Here are my mother's and aunt's names. Here is where my sister and I jousted with long sticks. Here is where I learned to drive. I practiced for cheerleading here and slept off Easter dinner here." I can see the church crumbling away. Fry St. a ghetto. Holiday Lanes closed and Dennys and Best Western gone forever.

And then I'd get that longing—longing for a home.

THE YEAR OF LIVING POETICALLY

Brian Polak

Least Likely to . . . Maintain a Noticeable
Amount of Happiness over a Significant
Amount of Time

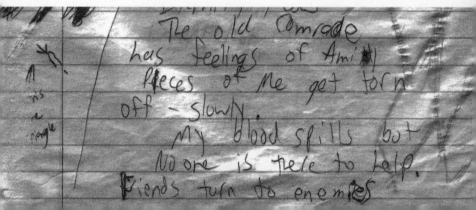

At fifteen I had all the necessary ingredients to be a great poet: low self-esteem, an influential friend, and an infatuation for a girl named Jocelyn. It was the perfect storm of teen angst.

My friend had me convinced that putting my feelings for Jocelyn on paper in the form of *poetry* was the best thing to do. Maybe it would even get her to pay attention to me.

I believed my friend to the tune of fifty poems over the course of one school year. I eventually grew bold enough to spell her name with my words, you know, so she would know they were about her if she ever read them. Even though she wouldn't give me the time of day, I tried really hard to remain positive.

HAPPY LIKE A CLOWN

You are the one I love the best
Your face picks me up when I'm down
I love you better than all the rest

You make me feel happy like a clown
I wish we could be together forever
But my battle for you is going downhill
We could be so good together
I have wished my love to be stronger than your will

I love most everything about you
I love you so much I wish you could see
The one thing that makes me feel blue
Is that you will never love me

NIGHTMARE

What I dream of is you loving me
You and I together—can you see?
What I love:
Your face
Your eyes
Do I know why?
What do you see
When you look into me?
Is it love?
Is it hate?
Tell me—I need to know my fate
You bring peace to my life of war

What should I do?
Should I stay?
Should I flee?
My darkest nightmare is you hating me

DREAM

Just what I want
Onset of love
Can't get too close
Endless time to wait
Life full of lies

Youth going to waste
Nobody cares

JACKPOT

You are the Jackpot
But you may not be mine I heard from the wise Owl
When I try to see or talk to you in would come the
Cobra and tear me away
My love is Eternal
It is a Living death being away from you
We are two Young bloods
Never to be together . . . Never

ADULT ME SAYS:

After fifty poems I gradually started to take the hint that maybe this relationship wasn't meant to be. Like many of the great poets before me, I became succinct and, moreover, bitter.

JOCELYN IS FAT

Jocelyn is fat
She sat on a rat
And that was the end of that

ADULT ME SAYS:

Eventually, she was shown the notebook. To this day I am uncertain whether or not she actually read any of the poems inside it.

Date 2 10/14/88 Sunday

Today Ema was
baptized. We
Christians.
Mom and
a valentine, a
plastic container
a heart lollipop.
valentines for everyone
Today Michael (my
pretend boyfriend) the

MY IMAGINARY VALENTINE
Karen Corday

Most Likely to . . . Write a Really Hot Story
and Circulate It Around Class

drove to my house
a motorcycle and I got on
the back. We soared off.
We got to a huge deserted
and. We glided into the
ice. I whirled into an

Growing up in rural New Hampshire, all I wanted to be was a glamorous, popular teenager. I was obsessed with all things teen, from the Sweet Valley High books (I preferred Jessica, the conniving, slightly slutty twin who all the boys loved) to *The Facts of Life* (featuring mean, impeccable Blair) to John Hughes movies (always taking special interest in the bitchy blond cheerleading babes with their hunky, adoring boyfriends).

As far as I could tell, the main activity practiced by teenage girls—besides putting on blue eye shadow and being incredibly mean to their supposed best friends—was having *boyfriends*. I started trying to conduct dramatic, doomed relationships with unwilling boys as soon as I entered elementary school. Of course my attempts at "dating" were met with confusion and terror.

By the time I got to sixth grade, I was so utterly frustrated with the lack of romance in my life that I invented an imaginary boyfriend named Michael as a Valentine's Day present . . . to myself.

February 14, 1988
Michael is my make-pretend boyfriend who only lives in my mind and diary. He's 14. Anyway, he called and asked me ice skating. So, he drove to my house on a

171

motorcycle and I got on the back. We soared off. We got to a huge deserted pond.

We glided onto the ice. I whirled into an intricate routine, and he skated in a circle around me. I did a perfect jump, came down, and landed in his arms! He skated for awhile, holding me. Then, he gently set me down. He raised my chin and whispered, "You're so beautiful."

The song "Stand By Me" came on out of nowhere. He took both my hands and we spun in a circle together. Just when I thought I could whirl no longer, we stopped. As Ben E. King climaxes into a passionate "So darlin', darlin' stand by me! Ohh, stand by me," we throw our lips together and kiss madly. We clutch each other as if life depended on it as the kiss deepens.

Finally, we part, only to repeat the process twice more. We twirl around awhile.

"We better go, gorgeous."

"Oh Michael! Stay with me!"

"Darling, I must take you back."

"I love you, Michael."

"And I love you! Oh damn! I love you so much!" (We kiss passionately for about five minutes. Our lips part.)

"Oh, Karen!" pants Michael.

"Michael!" I breath.

We kiss again.

And again.

"I wish we could spend forever together."

"Oh my precious Michael. Me too!"

"You're so perfect, Karen. I love everything about you."

"Oh Michael!"

ANOTHER long kiss.

"We better go."

We get on the motorcycle and drive home.

"See you soon, cutie!"

"Sure!" We kiss.

"I love you." (Both.)

He roars off.

THE END

CORPORAL PUNISHMENT

Jami Mandl

Most Likely to . . . Smoke Pot in the Woods
During Algebra

When I was eighteen, I couldn't wait to move out of the house. I packed up my clothes in a Hefty bag; took one plate, one fork, and one knife; and hopped on the El to move in with my friends Mary and Chris and their newborn, Carrie.

It was the early nineties. We were in the middle of the Gulf War, and George Bush (the father, not the son, and definitely not the Holy Spirit) was president. Mary and I were all fired up to go to protests, start petitions, and hang our NO BLOOD FOR OIL posters all over Chicago. We were going to single-handedly end the war!

Then I met the marine.

He was an old friend of Chris's, home on leave, soon to be discharged from the Marine Corps, and he needed a place to stay. The corporal and Chris moved into the second floor apartment, and Mary, the baby, and I took the apartment right above them. We all ended up sharing both apartments, which I came to call "the Duplex." This is my tale of misery.

DEC. 2nd

I don't feel so good. In fact, I feel shitty & extremely nauseous. I definitely have a fever, but I don't know how high because the only thermometer in this fucking apartment is Carrie's—i.e. RECTAL, NO THANK YOU! Maybe it's listening to George Bush talk about the Gulf War that's making me sick. Smarmy bastard!

Speaking of the war, my Corporal is coming upstairs later to hang out and hopefully spend the night. These living arrangements are almost too weird, even for me. Mary & I up here; Chris and the Corporal downstairs . . . one big dysfunctional family. Not too different from what most of us grew up in. Anyway, I'm really excited to see Corporal tonite, but what else is new? When he's not around I daydream about him—I can *smell* him. I can *feel* him. I can *taste* him. My yummy Marine . . . God I feel sick.

The last time we were together was sorta messed up because it was quarter beer night at the Pumping Company so we, of course, took advantage of it. It's nice living walking distance from a bar that doesn't check for I.D. I think it's the C cups that grant me entrance. Anyway, we all went down there, armed with a whole $5.00 each, and ready to drink! We passed our downstairs neighbor who I call Mr. Willy ever since I caught sight of him naked in his doorway—NOT GOOD! It was toooo gross.

I think I might throw up, really. BY THE WAY, *why* are we in Kuwait anyway? And how on Earth did I end up semi-dating a Marine? I could, and have, and will again, fill up notebooks about the why's and how's of our relationship. Oh shit, there's only 2 hours til he gets here!

So, Mr. Willy gives us this sorta freaked out look, like we're aliens. I guess we look sorta freaky as a group. Chris with his crazy black curls and combat boots; Mary with her wild red hair—also wearing combat boots, me with my short skirt, fishnets, ALSO wearing combat boots, and Corporal—the clean shaven Marine who, by the way, is also wearing combat boots. Funny, all of us ready for combat and only one Marine! We drank and drank and drank— I'm seriously ready to puke right now—and got back to the Duplex around 2:30. I was feeling all liquid-y and wobbly.

Mary and Chris go to the 2nd floor (Carrie was at Grandma's for the weekend) and Corporal and I go to the 3rd floor (God, these living arrangements really *are* fucked up!). We tripped over all the unpacked boxes laying around, and, of course, over all the GODDAMN cats. He wanted to listen to Kitaro . . . I *love* watching him. His body is sooooo fine—basic training was gooooood to him!

PREPARE FOR THE NEW WORLD ORDER! READ *MY* LIPS! I wonder if Bush's son was ever in the military? Well, now I can vote so hopefully next election we'll get a good President because . . . because what? I lost my train of thought. Oh, yes, my Marine with his beautiful brown eyes and those lips. Sometimes when he looks at me, *my bones melt*. I feel it from the top of my head to the tips of my toes . . . so easy to get distracted thinking about him! He put on Kitaro and lit some candles and some Champa incense. We were just talking, laughing; vibing on each other . . . he was twirling a lock of my hair around his fingers. He told me he thinks it's sexy when I bite my lip when I look at him. I almost wish he hadn't, because now, every time I do it, I'm like TOTALLY aware of it.

We were kissing and he just smelled SO good! Right in the middle of a kiss, my stomach rolled up in my throat and I tried to jump up and run into the bathroom, but since I was a little, well, a LOT drunk, that was difficult. I tripped over a kitty and puked all over the floor. It was SO gross! I finally made it to the bathroom and just kept barfing. He asked if I was O.K. a couple of times, and through mouthfuls of vomit I asked him to please just go home. I didn't hear him leave, but I KNOW he heard me! Now I have to jump in the shower because he'll be here soon. I wonder if we have any Tylenol or something?

DEC. 6th

Home from work. It's 9:15 and for once I have the place to myself. The guys are off playing Dungeons & Dragons somewhere. How come all the games they play involve killing? Doesn't being in the Marines satisfy that urge for Corporal? I doubt he'll come over tonight. He's probably freaked out and I am SO embarrassed. It never seems to end, the humiliating things that happen to me. The other night he showed up around 10:00 or so and I was still feeling icky. He had brought over some food and as soon as he started eating I got sick AGAIN, but at least I made it to the bathroom in time.

I knew I had the flu, or something, and I tried to explain that to him, but he just sat there with this icked out look on his face and said, "If you're sick, maybe I'd better go." I've gone from being the crazy, funny girl who bites her lip to the girl who pukes every time he comes around. Jesus Christ—maybe he'll forget about it. I won't—EVER! I'm just gonna lay low, listen to some Dead and try NOT to vomit.

DEC. 15th
Am feeling better and somewhat validated. All the puking and grossness was actually the result of a really bad kidney infection. No matter what the reason is, though, nothing about tossing your cookies not ONCE but TWICE in front of a hot guy is remotely appealing. This hospital is TOTALLY bogus and I want to go home! The day after my last vomit session with Corporal, my back was killing me and I had a high fever, so I dragged my sorry ass to St. Francis and here I've been ever since. I've found a partner in crime, though. This orderly, or attendant, or whatever they're called named Willie (coincidence??) gives me forbidden cigarettes. I unplug my stupid I.V. and smoke outside and nobody says anything.

Maybe because I look like a mental patient people stay away. The one person who has stayed FAR FAR away is Corporal. On the one hand, I understand—

the last 2 times we were together were hardly the romantic interludes I had envisioned, BUT COME ON! A little sympathy, please???? I still think he should've called or something.

Seriously, I watched Japanese animation with him for God's sake! The more I think about it, the more pissed I get. I mean, it's not like we're married or anything, but I am sort of his girlfriend, and sort of his roommate . . . all these "sort of's" are a little discouraging. Still, it wouldn't hurt him to pick up the phone and ask how I am, would it? At least I know I won't be dwelling in this all night. The little blue pills they hand out around 9:00 are *quite* lovely. O.K., so maybe what I need to do is distance myself from him a little—not easy living 5 stairs away from each other, but I'll try. Just be civil and do my thing. I'll keep him the same distance I keep Mr. Willy. Good plan!!

DEC 18th

Finally home! We're all supposed to get together tonite in the 2nd floor clubhouse to watch a movie. It'll be the first time I've seen Corporal since my return from kidney hell. I've been vomit free for a week and am ready to be in the same room and ignore him.

LATER: I am such a *SUCKER*! I was able to play it cool for about 15 minutes until he sat next to me on the couch, put his arm around me and whispered, "I missed you." Inside I was *raging* . . . MISSED ME? WHERE WERE YOU? A BIG BAD MARINE TOO

SCARED OF A LITTLE PUKE TO CALL OR VISIT?
NOT SUCH A TOUGH GUY AFTER ALL!

I really wanted to say all of this, but ended up
putting my head on his shoulder and said, "I missed
you, too." We snuggled on the couch and watched
some David Lynch movie. I wanted to be the strong,
independent woman I'm *supposed* to be, but instead
I become some doormat! Ah, but a doormat with a
hot Marine to cuddle with. When I woke up, he was
gone—POOF! He's very good at making a stealthy
getaway. Something he learned in the Marine Corps
maybe? He had some clothes piled on a chair, so I
grabbed a "Semper Fi" T-shirt to take home—I'll wear
it to bed and maybe have some sweet dreams.

DEC. something . . .
Haven't talked to Corporal for *days*. He did leave a
message on our machine, though—"Hey Jami, do you
have a shirt of mine? If you do, can you please bring it
back?" I cannot do anything right. There's no dignity
left in my life. I guess I'll have to suck it up and
return it. But what's my reason for taking it in the first
place? I have none. I'll go down and return it later. No
harm, no foul, hopefully.

LATER:
IT NEVER ENDS. I went downstairs, thinking he'd be
at work and I could give the shirt to Chris and avoid
dealing with the whole situation, BUT NO. Of course
not! Why should anything be that easy? Corporal

answers the door, looking sorta weird. I give him a big smile—"Here's your shirt" and waited for him to invite me in or something. He didn't.

Then I heard that Kitaro tape playing in the background and GODDAMMIT—I could smell the incense from the doorway! I also got a glimpse of a very short girl, with very long brown hair walking into the bathroom. It was soooo awkward—I didn't know what to say! I wanted to freak the fuck out and tell him that this stupid seduction scene doesn't work and that he should try some new material, but I couldn't. Probably because I wished it were me in there.

I don't even remember what dumb thing I said, I just sorta bolted back upstairs and paced around the apartment chain smoking. WHAT AN UTTER ASSHOLE! Doesn't Semper Fi mean always faithful or something like that? I will NEVER leave this apartment.

At least until I run out of cigarettes.

LATER:

The on-going saga of my crappy day has no end in sight. I went to get smokes and I was coming back in the building, out walks THAT GIRL wearing, what else? A fucking Semper Fi T-shirt. WHY IS SHE WEARING THAT?? I don't even want to think about it. I cannot think about it. I *do* think I will go upstairs and hang myself right now.

Or maybe I should just move.

saw me, but he didn't ack
my presence. It couldn't h
even he didn't want to lo
uncool in front of his fri
because he wasn't with
(He's a junior) That's another
he's so obsessed with
I mean, he
tries too
he's a je
he'd conc
coolness
hate his
brown eyes

HEAVY METAL HEARTACHE

Colleen Kane

Most Likely to . . . Draw Band Logos on
Notebooks

Glen Molinary, and he's in
really cool band, Hit & R
Well Patricia Cardinali jus
me today that he told r
about sleeping with his g
friend (He's 18 or 19). I co
believe it! For some rea
I couldn't imagine it ar

Throughout my teen years in suburban New Jersey, I loved me some long-haired rock-and-rollers. It started in 1984 at age ten.

I felt the first spark watching David Lee Roth in the video for Van Halen's "Jump," yet to innocent, shame-filled, Irish Catholic me my interest in Diamond Dave seemed dangerous and bad.

A few years later the still just as innocent and shame-filled me could no longer resist, and Bon Jovi's seminal 1986 album *Slippery When Wet* opened the floodgates. I was as supremely obsessed as only a teenage girl in love can be.

It didn't matter that my love was unrequited. Teenage girls don't require reciprocation. They can exist for months on the vapors of a single interaction with the object of desire.

Still, I dreamed of the day when I'd have a hot headbanger boy of my own. No mall was too large. No concert was too motley. I was determined to find him. I would leave no stoner unturned.

September 28, 1988

I am friends with this guy Glen, and he's in this really cool band, Hit & Run. Well Patricia just told me today that he told her about sleeping with his girlfriend

(He's 18 or 19). I couldn't believe it! For some reason I couldn't imagine it and especially telling Patricia about it. I don't know why. I just thought he'd have better morals. Maybe I'm a prude. Nah!

November 20, 1988
Dear Diary,

I'm in love! I like this junior Jack who's a drummer in Glen's band, which is now called Matrix. He is SO hot! He has long blond hair. Mom doesn't trust him because of his long hair. Anyway, I found out he works at Pathmark so I will conveniently start to work there. AND GUESS WHAT?!?!?! He <u>called</u> last night (this morning) at 12:30!!!! He called to talk to Sean. Mom answered (it woke her up—I would have gladly answered had I been awake!) She told him Sean doesn't take calls after 12:00!!! Then she HUNG UP on him!!!! I could've died.

This morning when she told us at breakfast, I thought I was still dreaming! I almost worked up my courage today to stop him in the hall and apologize for Mom's behavior.

Almost. But he wasn't there anyway.

December 12, 1988
I've made up my mind to use visualization as this week's method for trying to become Jack's girlfriend. I've tried prayer, being introduced by Patricia, and next I'll try going to the practice of his band, Matrix. At the Amnesty concert at school Sat. nite, they were

SOOO awesome. Mark my words—Jack will be a famous drummer someday.

He isn't.

Feb 23, 1989

DUDE! I got Jack's drumstick!!!

Me & Patty went to see Blind Ambition (the band's new name) at Obsessions, a club with a young adults night. It was awesome. Jack was wearing a cropped white shirt and holey jeans with leopard shorts underneath. He looked SOOOOOOOOOOOOO HOT! Wait til I tell Denise S.! She would be too shy to pick up the stick off the stage like I did. Actually the stick hit me in the head when Jack threw it from behind his red drum set (the stick was broken) then landed on the stage. I didn't know what hit me, but I grabbed it! It was still warm from his amazing hands when I got mine on it.

I'm sleeping with the stick under my pillow tonight and every night from now on. It'll be sure to give me pleasant dreams! (about Jack, of course!) I'm so lucky! In another second one of those other vultures would have gotten MY drumstick. I happened to be at the right place at the right time.

ADULT ME SAYS:

After coasting on that high for two months, I went to my

first Bon Jovi concert at the Brendan Byrne Arena, and a few months after that I went to their even bigger concert at Giants Stadium. I took a week to write a full report, which was about ten notebook pages long, front and back. Here's a much-abbreviated version.

June 14, 1989

The Concert Was SOOOOOOOOOOO Awesome!

I wore my Bon Jovi shirt, black jeans, mirrored shades, waved my hair. I must say I looked quite good.

We finally got there at 4. As we walked from the parking lot we saw tons of people—mostly teens, mostly bleached-blonde girls and longhaired guys wearing Bon Jovi shirts and mostly black or ripped jeans. And leather. There were lotsa tailgate parties in the parking lot. Lotsa drinking and people were burning something. . . .

We wove through the crowd—so many people! And even more came—many, MANY hot guys . . .

Sam Kinison came on with his sluts in g-strings and skimpy bras and screamed about being in Jersey (crowd: YAAAAAAAA! Whenever Jersey was mentioned, everyone screamed their heads off including me)
. . .

Skid Row came on! I must explain something. Denise and Michelle sort of hate Skid Row so I didn't really let loose and party to them. Patty likes them though. . . . They ended their set with "Youth Gone Wild." Duders!

We found a way to get right up front! Billy Squire came on (who?) and ended. We began our long (about an hour or two) wait for Bon Jovi. As we waited, several interesting things happened. Security hosed us down! It was hot in the sun, but not really in the shade of the stage. All around me I could smell hair spray on wet hair! Well, there goes MY hair.

We saw an absolute CLONE of Jon Bon Jovi. I think it might have been his brother! He had a girlfriend with him but I noticed him looking at me out of the corner of his eye a few times! It def wasn't JBJ though, altho' denise contended so. His eyes were brown, his chest wasn't hairy enough, his face didn't have the slightest trace of stubble and it was still kinda—not chubby, but not as skinny as JBJ's. I really think it was his brother.

Also this girl got on the shoulders of her bf wearing this teeny skimpy top. No bra, of course. She went to pull it up a bit and all the guys started hooting and catcalling because it looked like she was taking it off. Ya know what? She DID! The slut!

Well, she just pulled it up to flash her boobs at the guys after they kept prompting her. Her bf turned her all around so everyone could get a good view. Believe me, they all did. Then she was brought back up several more times and every time she did all the guys yelled for her to take off her top and she was always like "No no no well OK." All the girls were like, what a slut! That was the extent of our waiting entertainment.

The show started! I can't pinpoint the exact moment that the members of BJ came on stage, all of a sudden there was a collective scream, lurch toward the stage as the music started. The song was "Lay Your Hands on Me." I watched on the two giant screens Jon salute the crowd, with so much emotion in his eye. As the show progressed we got closer and closer to the stage. It was awesome. It was a rock n roll dream. It was the Woodstock of the 80s. I know I'll never forget that afternoon and evening. I remember looking at the crowd and thinking, "It doesn't get any better than this." I bet Bon Jovi was thinking the same thing.

The best part maybe of Bon Jovi's set was before the song "Blood on Blood." Jon gave this little talk about life not being just getting from point A to point B. You gotta have dreams, whether it be a rock and roll star or President of the United States. And no matter what that dream is, you can make it come true! I was one hair away from crying. Many around me were. Mary S. told me she did. You see, that talk really hit home with me. At that moment, Jon Bon Jovi was practically God.

There were many more awesome songs, most from the *New Jersey* album, and I was dancing and singing my head off. Patty would scream so loud every once in awhile that I could feel my hearing being damaged. My ears rang for about a week later. Then Skid Row, Billy Squier, and Sam Kinison

came out for a semi-finale, round of "Wild Thing."
Sam Kinision screaming it his way, JBJ singing it the
original way, letting us repeat him. The group's really
into audience participation.

. . .

The end was firework-filled, and we were about
5 feet from the stage! Then it was over. It was sort of
a relief (only a tiny bit) because I was so tired. That
concert WAS New Jersey that day.

The next day about 39 people asked me how the
concert was and I told 'em it was SO awesome, but
they couldn't understand because they weren't there. I
MISS EVERYTHING!

September 4, 1989

Oh my gosh! So much has happened since I got a
perm! Thursday, I got my perm and was really scared,
but it came out looking really nice and I look *older*
now. Friday, I'd been at Denise A's overnight and that
day we went to Great Adventure.

Two guys tried to pick us up—real geekaroos.
Well one was OK. But the scuzz, Carl, was a showoff,
and he tried to start a conversation with us by
commenting on my Bon Jovi shirt. He said "Bon Jovi
stinks." (LIES!) I turned around and glared at him.
His cousin, as I learned he was later, was apologetic.
He's like, "I like Bon Jovi." I turned back around. Carl,
(no, I bet it's spelled the annoying way, with a K) Karl
continued. "No, they really do."

I turned, glanced at his Ozzy Ozbourne t-shirt,

and said, "Ozzy sucks." His cousin, Mike, said, I agree, "Ozzy does suck, and Bon Jovi's cool."

I thanked him, and Denise & I went on the Ferris wheel. Then after the ride the guys hooked up with us and came along to the Scream Machine. Embarrassing. What could we say? Go away?

That night we went to the boardwalk. We saw these guys a few times as we walked up and down and one with long brown hair was pretty cute. They said hello once as we passed. Then when waiting for our pictures to come out of the booth, one of the guys that had said hello asked me if I'd like to meet that guy over there and asked my name.

He went over to the long-haired (!) guy and told him, came back and told me his name was Mike, went back, and brought Mike and his friends and we, Denise, Mike & I walked off. We talked basically about music and Bon Jovi. He's really nice and really sweet and cute. Not hot, but cute. So after about an hour, his friends told him they had to go home.

So he had to go, but he asked for my #! He had me write it on the back of a picture he'd won of a naked woman with strategically placed limbs and beer bottle. Classy.

After that, Denise and I freaked! She was so psyched for me! Then we walked to a private part at the boardwalk and she told me about this guy who'd been calling her for awhile and I touched the sand because I hadn't touched it all summer. It was so soft.

It was a starless night, as Mike had pointed out. Then we went home.

We've talked on the phone 4x, a record for me. He really likes talking to me. It's a toll call. He wants to spend all his money on calling me! He wants to ride his bike to my house! (He lives 1/2 an hour from Point Pleasant) And—he told me I'm pretty!!!!! EEEEEEEEEEEEEEEEEEEE! This is the first time a boy ever has!

. . .

Well, as you can imagine, my confidence is really boosted—one reason that I'm sorta looking forward to school. I think the guys'll notice me this year, if Friday was any indication. Well, I'm gonna go brood over some cookies and milk. Bye.

I am writing this diary because I don't ever want to forget these years of my life and maybe some-day I'll base a book on, it!

I NEED A HERO

Sean Sweeney

Most Likely to . . . Succeed at Very Little

When I was eleven, twelve, and thirteen years old, I felt like I just wasn't getting laid as much as I thought I should be. I wanted to be the coolest independent dude who everybody listened to and to have hot chicks dig me. Everything I wasn't.

Since reality wasn't in my favor, I decided I would write a screenplay (or what I thought was one) where these wishes came true.

It was inspired by *Lord of the Flies*. We had to read the novel for school. I only got through the first ten pages, but I stared at its cover for hours. I just thought it would be a better book if it had someone, well, someone more like me in it.

```
"Apocoliptic Island"
By
```
Sean Sweeney
Coming soon to a movie theater near you.
Starring Al Pacino, Debra Winger, Roy Scheider,
Phoebe Cates
And Sean Sweeney
"The best movie of the year" —Sneak Previews
Winner of 4 Academy Awards

Scene 1: Boat Scene
The boat carries the school class.

Scene 2
On the island a bunch of people survived the boat crash. Shawn, a pretty good-looking teen, the kinda guy normal girls may NOT think is hot, but smart types of girls who like stuff—who live in New York or Paris and maybe model sometimes, like him. People think he's funny or cool. But he's like James Dean, deep. Maybe he pretends stuff is funny, but really he's sad.

ADULT ME SAYS:

That's Shawn, S-H-A-W-N. No relation to me, S-E-A-N.

Scene 3
Everyone finds food and makes a fire. Shawn takes pieces of the boat and makes a cool house shack.

Scene 4
People are scared. Shawn calms them down.

Some racist guys start to pick on this old black couple calling them "N***rs" and "Jiggaboos." Shawn takes a stick and fights both of them. He makes them say they are sorry.

The old black couple are happy. They give Shawn some apples.

ADULT ME SAYS:

Apparently one Scene 4 was just not enough.

Scene 4

Lisa is a hot mixed girl (like Lisa Bonet). She says she is the old couple's granddaughter.

Lisa: Thank you

Shawn: No problem

Lisa: Where are your parents?

Shawn: They died

Lisa: Are you sad?

Shawn: No.

They go to Shawn's hut and have to wash their dirty clothes. They start French-kissing and making out. She totally likes Shawn. She kisses him all over and starts to go down there.

Lisa: Do you want me to?

Shawn: Yeah baby it feels good.

They totally have sex.

(If its okay to get a R rating, maybe Lisa shows her boobs and butt. And Shawn shows his butt too . . . If PG just her butt.)

Scene 5

She lights a cigarette.

Lisa: Do you want one?

Shawn: I don't smoke, well not cigarettes.

Lisa: Do you smoke weed?

Shawn: Are you a cop?

Lisa: No.

Shawn: Then yeah.

Lisa: You got some?

Shawn: I bet it grows on this island.

Lisa: You're my first lover. I'll never forget it. It was so hot—I had so many orgasms.

Scene 6
People start screaming.
Shawn puts on just some shorts and Lisa puts on a
bikini.
They run to the people.
They see a boat sailing by.

ADULT ME SAYS:

I'm not sure if that was the end, or if I just got bored and
stopped writing.

But I think I was sad about having to leave the island
and having to go back to being Sean, S-E-A-N.

STAIRWAY TO WINNIPEG

Johanna Stein

Least Likely to . . . Make Deadlines

In eighth grade I had a huge hard-on for Pasquale Pescatore. He was a gorgeous Italian guy with long eyelashes and soccer legs. He loved head-banging music and threw weekend parties where everyone got trashed, and if you were a girl, you stood a very good chance of getting felt up.

I, on the other hand, played cello in the orchestra.

I signed up for guitar class, because that's where Pasquale hung out. I deduced that he would fall in love with me after witnessing my sexy badass guitar skills. But Pasquale skipped guitar class most days, so he missed seeing my axe skills.

Then one fateful day our social studies teacher, Mr. Pelisek, assigned us all to report on the history of our hometown, Winnipeg, Manitoba, Canada. Pasquale was in the class, so I decided to kill two birds with one stone and wrote a "poem" (in scented pen), setting it to the coolest song I could play on guitar.

I serenaded the entire class, hoping to finally win over Pasquale.

STAIRWAY TO WINNIPEG
(sung to the tune of "Stairway to Heaven")

Red River Colony
Was started by
Thomas Douglas,
He was the fifth
Earl of Selkirk
A noble-man.

Thomas Douglas
Was so rich
He dedicated
Himself
To helping all the crofters being driven from their
land.

Ooh ooh oooh ooh ooh ooh
Oooh ooh ooh ooh ooh ooh
Being driven to make room
For the sheep farms

He went to
Prince Edward Island
And in 1803
He established a colony
Of settlers

This plan worked out
Quite well

But he planned
To meet the settlers
But got delayed
Because of his
Private affairs

OOOH
STAIRWAY TO WINNIPEG
OOH
STAIRWAY TO WINNIPEG

When he finally arrived
He found all of the settlers
Living like Indians
And in wigwams

The next year
He sent more
Than 100 highlanders
To settle in Baldoon
In Upper Canada

OOOH STAIRWAY TO WINNIPEG
OOH STAIRWAY TO WINNIPEG

But this plan
Didn't work
As the land was too wet
And almost half of the settlers
Died of disease

LA LA LA LA LA LA LA LAAAA

During the climax of the song, I was shredding away on my nylon-stringed guitar. I looked at the sea of faces in class. My friends. Mr. Pelisek. And yes, Pasquale—he finally noticed me!

They stared back at me with an expression which at the time I believed was admiration and awe, but in retrospect was clearly horror and revulsion.

BIG FINALE:
Red River Colony
Went through so
Many changes
And is now the nucleus
of Winnipeg

PARENTS JUST DON'T UNDERSTAND

R.P.

Least Likely to . . . Stop Being Bubbly

I grew up with strict, controlling parents who never let me do much. I wasn't allowed to stay up late, talk to boys on the phone, or go to slumber parties. Nothing. Sometimes I'd run out and dive into a moving car when my friends picked me up, so my parents wouldn't see who I was with. I pretty much did what I was told, and things were okay.

But then I met Bill . . . and that's when I started fighting with my parents. I was fourteen, and all I really wanted was some freedom. A suburban Romeo and Juliet.

My dad was very overdramatic. But so was I, which is something you might pick up on from the multiple death threats made toward my family members. But just to reassure you, the reader, everyone is still alive and well.

Dearest Alyssa,
Hey there you! I'm listening to my CD of Celine Dion and I set the songs to "All by Myself" and "Call the Man." Guess what song is on right now? "All by Myself." But that's okay, right? I swear I must sound fucking delirious or something and here I am listening to this song and crying. Oh did I mention that when I called Bill the ninth time my mom starting bitching at me again about having a boyfriend and because I was already pissed off I yelled, "Maybe I should tell dad

about all the bills you hide" and I know I hit a soft spot because she started bitching about how stressed her life is and shit. WHATEVER! She can threaten all she wants because I sure as fuck am not afraid of her short fat ass.

Well Boo-Boo I feel a little better typing the fucking shit out of my keyboard. Don't trip if I kill anyone I know you won't snitch on me. I'm kidding of course, I wouldn't kill anyone . . . just kidding. Well I'll talk to you and see you around or whatever whenever. Night-night!

Dear Diary,
There was another blackout. Dad was yelling at me for going to sleep cuz Daniel was screaming for a Capri Sun. But the bastard . . .

ADULT ME SAYS:

My dad.

. . . that thing, he came into the house tracking mud all over the kitchen tiles and threatening to smash my face unless I cleaned it up properly! I didn't think about running away again. Just running like I always do. My fastest way to freedom. All I thought about was killing them. The two fuckers who lived inside the room down the hall.

My parents.

I would kill him by shooting him and enjoying watching him squirm. He deserved it. I could easily cover it up. I bet I could. And her . . . I would probably keep locked up somewhere till she died of starvation. She could get skinny the way she wanted to. Oh well.

I hurt Daniel again today. I didn't beat him with my bare hands this time. I tried to suffocate him with a pillow. But I stopped, I always stop. He's only four and yet he still goes through the same hell we all do.

Dearest Bill,
I'm not going to Grad Nite, anymore. I decided to risk fighting for my right as a senior and I butted heads with a selfish father. My dad compares me to every girl that is televised on TV. My dad threatened to kick me out of the house because I wanted to go. He said all I'm doing is disobeying him and because of that I need to "pack your things and leave the house" and I don't need to call him "Daddy" anymore. This was all caused because a part of the waiver

Permission slip

he had to sign stated that he would be responsible for my actions. In his mind he said, "When your bus rolls off a bridge I'm liable for the damages! As a parent you don't know how I feel stupid." No I'm stupid, along with my mom because she can't read. My dad is using examples from TV again; Christina Williams being kidnapped, a girl in a Santa Rosa prom that got drunk and was raped, three women that got stuff in a trunk and got burned. He's continuing on and on. I'm sitting here in tears and he's threatening to not send me to college. My dad says if I want to go out so much I should get out of this house. You know what he says, "I am worse than a devil. The devil is afraid of me!" My dad is mad because of the waiver he has to sign, he believes that the school is double crossing him. Will I ever be freed from his tyranny?

Dearest Bill,
I'm back and my dad is being a bitch again. He blew up out of nowhere! Threatening to hang Samuel, then looking at me and then saying, "This house of full of animals." It started when Daniel stole Dragon Ball Z and Robby got annoyed, I turned off the Super Nintendo. My mom started bitching at both me and Robby, "You better watch out, he's observing you." Then Daniel started throwing stuff and then my dad went off. It had its suddenness as usual, but it was the surprise that he had cables in his hands when he threatened to hang Daniel that caught me off guard.

Oh well. He rushes into the kitchen like that

saying he has mental problems. Ok! I hope Friday
is safe enough for us to see one another. I hate my
parents, they're only around to screw up my life.
I'm marrying you whether he or anyone else has a
problem. Please remember that you're always in my
heart. Good night and I await you in my dreams.
Your everything and more,
R

My asshole of a father hates you?!

Dear love of mine Bill,
Hello there darling! I told my dad that I called you
and that I was talking to you. Yes, he got very pissed.
He said I should be "ashamed for calling a guy," he'll
"duck tape your mouth to the phone," and I should
"leave the house and never come back." He hates his
life and something about cutting off his hand?! Oh
well.

    I'm sorry for the distance again. If my home life
wasn't so fucked I'd be fine. I miss you so much.
You take me away from my prison, only you can slip
through the gates of my cage. My asshole of a father.
But I love you more than anything regardless of what
he thinks. You carry the key to my heart and I trust
you with my soul. My life is so much better when I
have you. For the 9 months we've been together, I
can't see any reason for being away from you. Wait for
me ok? Wait until I can be set free.

This Romeo and Juliet story has a happy ending. Bill and I never took the poison. And after ten long years, we've stayed together, even though we kept our relationship a secret even through college. I eventually did get out of my house and never killed anyone.

Harassmen[...]
[...]y day. A group of teenage [...]
girl tries to make her way to class. [...]
[...]vious stares, and endless calls of "Yeah, I'd [...]
like a slap in the face to the girl. While she was[...]
[...]ttacked, the boys' actions might as well be an assault
[...]heir behavior would make anyone feel embarassed,
[...]violated. This everyday occurance in high schools used
[...]ed. Parents, teachers, and [...] simply surrendered
that this type of harassm[...]le. Today,
[...]ople are beginning to re[...]
[...] and should be stopped.
Some people still call se[...]
Webster's Dictionary cal[...]
[...]someone". While it is tr[...]
[...]r comments about[...]
[...]believe t[...]

SEXUAL HARASSMENT ESSAY

Carrie Seim

Most Likely to . . . Have Her First Kiss at
Engineering Camp

[...]se their han[...]
[...]esirable girls in schoo[...]
[...]evaluation of girls creates an at[...]
learning and should not be tolerated in scho[...]
More and more, people are realizing that th[...]
behavior is unacceptable. The excuse of "boys will be
[...]should be able to handle a little teasing is not a va[...]
[...]should be taught to respect each other at a [...]
[...] Thomas had learned this lesson
[...]urt for sexual haras[...]

When I was growing up I wanted, more than anything, to be recognized as a great writer. A brilliant young woman with something powerful to say. And nothing gave me a bigger thrill than reading my material in front of others. But for some reason my public speeches never worked out quite as I imagined. In retrospect, it's clear I didn't understand two critical writing rules:

1. Write for your audience. (I preferred to write *against* my audience.)

2. Write what you know. (I never wrote about anything I had actually experienced.)

So when my seventh-grade English teacher asked us to write an essay about an injustice we had experienced personally, I naturally chose sexual harassment. This despite the fact that I wasn't exactly popular with the boys. I wore oversized glasses, a freakishly bad perm, and color-coordinated *skorts* and tights. The only time boys spoke to me was during our after-school engineering club.

This is the essay I wrote and read *out loud* in front of my entire English class. As you can guess from the photo, sexual harassment was a huge problem for me.

Sexual Harassment in High School
by Carrie Seim

It happens every day. A group of teenage boys gathers near the restroom as a lone girl tries to make her way to class. The boys' noisy whistles, obvious stares and endless calls of, "Yeah, I'd like to do that!" feel like a slap in the face to the girl. While she was not physically attacked, the boys' actions might as well be an assault on the girl.

Girls should not have to come to school knowing that they will be looked up and down by half of the math class every time they raise their hands, or wonder how they ranked on a "Pa-dow!"

ADULT ME SAYS:

Quick clarification. A "Pa-dow" was a list of the most desirable girls in school. Also note that the alleged harassment takes place in a *math* class.

All children should be taught to respect each other at an early age. Perhaps if Clarence Thomas had learned this lesson as a boy, he wouldn't have been taken to court for sexual harassment in the workplace.

It is the girls themselves who are often left with the problem of how to stop this harassment. Creating a list of the most desirable boys in school, or cat-calling after some attractive male is not a solution, or even a pleasant thought, for most girls.

All men should realize that coming to terms with women as real people and not fantasies is a part of growing up.

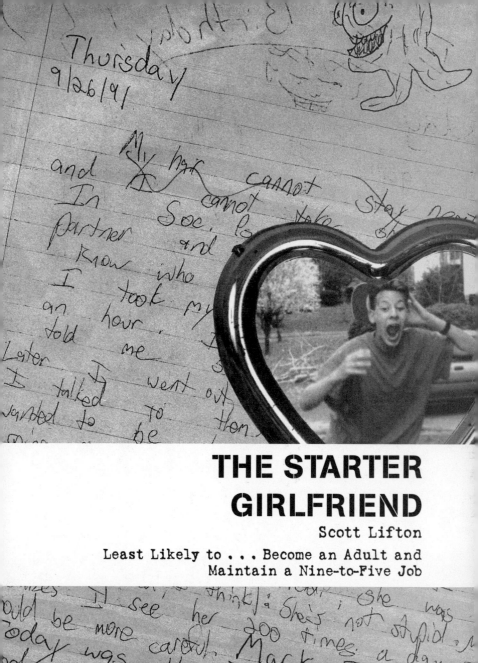

THE STARTER GIRLFRIEND

Scott Lifton

Least Likely to . . . Become an Adult and
Maintain a Nine-to-Five Job

This is from my diary when I was fifteen and sixteen. Back then, I was a little behind the times. My friends were starting to date, and I had yet to. I had a huge crush on the most popular girl in school. But I had no chance of getting her, and I really wanted a girlfriend.

So I ended up dating the first girl who showed me *any* attention at all. That's why you'll see my dramatic transition from giddy high school boy to asshole prick bastard in what follows.

Monday 9/30
During Study Hall me and Missy talked. Throughout the whole period. We're really good friends now. Good.

Saturday 10/19
Missy called at 9. We talked til 10. We both love *Grease 2* and are scheduled to see it next Saturday. I was thinking about her all day. It's weird . . . I want to spend every second with her, but I don't want to have sex with her or see her naked.

ADULT ME SAYS:

That should have been the first sign.

I don't know if I just want to be friends if I don't find her attractive or what?

Sunday 10/20
Ooh boy. These are confusing times. I am so mixed about Missy. I think of her all the time. I don't think she goes out though. I mean she's never been at the mall.

Monday 10/21
Oh God. Missy is really . . . I think about her about 90% of the time. Things are pretty intense. She talked about me and her going on cruises till we're 70. She's coming over Friday. I have to clean up.

Friday 10/25
IMPORTANT DAY IN HISTORY!! Yes it's true. I asked Missy out and she said yes. Well let's recap. She came home with me on the bus. We walked the dog and wrestled and stuff. My mom came home and made us English muffin pizzas as we watched *Heathers*. Both of us were lying on one couch hugging. I think I should sleep now. I feel kinda sick. Maybe it's Love.

Saturday 10/26
Ah . . . married life. I went to Missy's and brought *Grease 2*, *Outsiders* and chicken littles. We had fun. I tried to kiss her once. It didn't work. I don't know if I kissed her cheek or nose. It was kind of embarrassing

but I just laughed and said I slipped. I can't believe
we haven't even kissed yet. It's so nice though, lying
down, having her on top of me.

Sunday 10/27
Second Day Anniversary. Before, I was thinking
that I didn't want to be going out with Missy.
Responsibilities and crap . . . y' know? But I know
now that I definitely am glad.

Thursday 10/31 Halloween
We still haven't fucking kissed yet. There were 3 times
when I felt she was going to or maybe I would but
didn't. If we don't kiss soon, it'll be a big deal.

Saturday 11/2 IMPORTANT DAY IN HISTORY
I French kissed Missy. Finally!! We watched *Nightmare
on Elm Street* and *Saturday Night Live*. We kissed twice.
She hurt her nose and I went to kiss it and then
after that, I frenched her. It was only for like 7 or 8
seconds. Our teeth kept crashing.

Sunday 11/17
I feel bad for ignoring Todd last night but I was
horny . . . so passionate. Me and Missy both were . . .
we couldn't separate from each other. Our kisses are
so wet though it's starting to piss both of us off. Our
faces were hurting today. Probably from dried saliva.

Thursday 11/7

Ohh, I love Missy. I mean there's certain things which I hate about her. Her refusal to see *Star Wars, Batman* and other movies. Her hatred for cheese. But I just love her. Sometimes I'm with her and I just want to squeeze her and kiss her hard. It just felt really good to just lie on top of her.

Monday 11/8

I thought I'd go a day without seeing Missy . . . but I was wrong. We watched *Coming to America*. We kissed quite a few times and I think I'm really good at it now. I've been thinking though . . . do I want to go out with this girl for the rest of my high school career? She has no interest in sex or drinking. I mean we have a lot in common and there's a lot we don't have in common. Why be linked to one commonality?

But I can't break up with her. But I'm really glad I'm going out with her but I'm looking too far ahead. I'm only 16. Chill.

Saturday 11/9

I bought the *Robin Hood* video tape today. Then I went to Missy's. We kiss a little more often. We kissed once very hard for like a minute or two. I feel like I'm getting worse at kissing. Maybe the rhythms off. I think she knows it. I think I even hear her say it once. She opens her mouth too wide. I guess it's not really time to go up her shirt or down her pants or anything.

Wednesday 11/16

I just got off the phone with Missy and I'm kind of troubled. We had a first fight. She was watching the news and some twin babies died. She just said to hold on while she watched it and she told me that she's so depressed now. I was like . . . so? Do you know how many babies die a day? Do you know what else happens in the world? And I asked if she felt sorry for all the guys that died in Nam. She was shocked. She was like "You're so insensitive! How can you kid about death?"

I don't know about her but I don't take death very seriously and I don't think anyone should. After all, if she can't take a joke . . . I'm getting too far ahead of myself. I'm worrying about the relationship. I could never break up with her. Maybe this just showed me that our relationship isn't perfect and hunky dory.

Still she's one of those people who's really hooked on babies and I'm not. All I said was that the parents shouldn't have gotten upset because they didn't know the baby too long. It would've been worse had it been a 16 year old. I'm probably overdoing it. I'm too sensitive. That's my problem. Oh well. I gotz to go!

Thursday 11/17

I'm concerned about Missy. Missy's all pissed and she's been getting like that a lot lately. She gets angry and she just can't get rid of the anger. I think she needs a psychiatrist. Well I mean everyone does. Steven sure does. Todd and Ed too. Especially David. Everyone but me. Oh well.

Monday 11/18

I'm pissed now. Not pissed but confused. Every time I'm not with Missy I always think about the problems in our relationship. Why go steady with someone in high school unless you're getting married to them? You're only young once, you should go out and enjoy it. I like Missy but I know that I don't want to marry her and I feel trapped. How could I ever dump Missy? She would be crushed and she so doesn't deserve it. She's never done anything wrong to me. But I want to be with other people. It is high school. I am so confused.

Tuesday 11/19

I talked to Missy. I made a remark about how her and Tammy are like lesbians because they're buying each other rings. She went off and got really pissed. Well I really have to rethink dumping her. I basically know that this probably won't be a permanent relationship (I don't think we'll get married is what I mean) because we have too many differences. Oh well, nature calls.

ADULT ME SAYS:

What followed two weeks later was one of the world's worst breakups. It was full of clichés and lots of stuttering:

228

"It's not you; it's me . . . umm, ummm . . . I need space . . . ummm I still want to be friends . . . no, I really mean it . . . ummm."

I've gotten much better since then. I'm actually happy in love now. We love *each other*—I think it works better that way.

Amy forever. I really have nothing much more to say + I'm really tired so I digress.

word
to
your
mother

BREAKUP POETRY

Boni Joi

Least Likely to . . . Marry My High School
Sweetheart and Have Three Kids

Billy and I fell in love in eighth-grade math class. He had a blond bowl cut and looked like one of the Bad News Bears. We would stare at each other from across the room and he would wink at me slowly. We didn't really talk much, but we did a lot of kissing. Soon that wasn't enough for Billy. He kept trying to go to second base and wouldn't listen to me when I said no. So I broke up with him, thinking he would realize his mistake and proclaim his love.

Of course, I never told him why I was breaking up with him. I just wrote poems instead. Our breakup constituted most of the relationship.

After ninth grade I moved away, and I never saw Billy again. A few years ago my former BFF called and told me Billy was in jail for shooting at a cop. The policeman was my friend's ex, the one who took her virginity. They were both named Billy. Maybe if I had let him feel my teenage breasts he wouldn't have gone astray.

Untitled
I want you to know how I feel,
To tell you that my love is real,
You know a broken heart will
never heal.

Just one thing before you go,
Only one thing I want you to know,
My love for you is an endless flow.

If you were ever to leave me,
    What would I do?
I know I could never live with-
    out you.
Be mine forever, I really need you!

Don't Leave Me
How could you leave me when
You know I love you?
How could you leave me when
you know it's true?
How could you leave me I
Really need you?
What am I talking about?
    I'm leaving you.

Yesterday
Yesterday we were together.
Yesterday we had each other.
Yesterday was so much better.
Today I wish it were yesterday.

Hope
I hope the new day will bring
    sunshine;
But I know life isn't all

roses and honey.
I hope we will meet again . . .
    someday;
But I have this feeling we'll go
our own ways.
I hope one day things will be
    better for us,
And I know that day will
    come sooner or later.
I hope it's sooner.

Remembering

For Billy

Remembering visions of you in the
shadows of my dark eyes.
I felt so sad when you didn't
    understand,
because you were stubborn and
I just couldn't tell you how I
    felt.
It was like you were afraid to
    say goodbye;
so you made me say it.
I didn't really want to, but you
made me feel I had to . . .
You couldn't make me happier,
the way you smiled at me!
But one day that smile turned
    into a frown.
When I was down, you stepped

on me . . .
So I stepped on you,
I felt it was the right thing
    to do . . .
And still it's so hard for
me to forget about you!

Alone (A Song)

When you're alone all your life
    you need someone to turn to.
When you're alone all your life
    you have no one to turn to . . .
And I thought that when I met you,
Billy, I would be able to turn to you.
But some things in life
They just don't come true.

Well I've been this way
All of my life . . .
Livin' and Lovin' but
    never feeling right.
When you're this way
All of your life
It's hard to relate to someone.
But telling you my feelings, Billy,
    that's a start.

HOT FOR TEACHER

Marnie Pomerantz

Least Likely to . . . Win a National Scrabble
Tournament

My journal is filled with entries about the love of my life, during my senior year in high school . . . my teacher, Mr. Brent Perkins, aka BP. With graduation coming up in June, I knew I wouldn't be seeing him every day anymore.

So my goal was to chronicle everything—every moment between us, every minute detail. I didn't write it in my usual matter-of-fact style. My thinking was that if he ever found my diary—say, in the lunchroom, or years later when we were married— I wanted him to think that I was a literary *genius*, the next Dostoyevsky or Emily Dickinson. I even drew him.

MR. P.

"B.P."

MAY 15th

When I look back on my day, I see myself walking
onto the campus grounds in a silk pink tank top,
khaki shorts and my rock 'n roll belt. It's impulse now,
walking up the stairs and into the main building,
passing the principal's office on the left and the
Admissions office on the right and then, like a magnet
I am pulled right past the Switchboard and into *his*
office. There, Mr. Perkins lives his role, plays his part
in his life. I plop down in his chair and wait for him
to come back from the auditorium. Oh! I desperately
hope he comes back soon. Even if he doesn't, I still
enjoy . . . just sitting here, once again . . . in the nest
of youth.

MAY 21st

It sounds obscene that I am in love with him. Who
am I? Where is Marnie? She seems to be drowning in
all of this fear and love and passion. I am gasping for
breath. I miss him soooooooooo much. But, he led
me on in such a strange way. His words, his eyes, they
spoke a different language than I'd ever known. God,
I wonder if he had to take a lie detector test, would
he reveal his inner most emotions? What does he
truly think of me? I will never know. It will never be
clear, lucid. He loves to make the ambiguity painful;
he likes potent chaos within my brain. He is selfish,
unfair, and cruel! But, how? He opened my mind . . . I
was on honor roll for two semesters for him. I caused
the confusion myself. I am the guilty, fucked up

one—tainted by my strange relations with men.

Will I ever be normal, or will I always cause other males to bring out their bad qualities, which in turn, destroy me and my identity? I am reading Henry Miller's *Tropic of Cancer*, and I have to get back to my book. THE CLOCK OF LOVE HAS STOPPED FOR ME!

ADULT ME SAYS:

I stayed after school every day in the hope that he would let me drive him home. Two days a week I was able to badger him into it. We were in my car together for thirty minutes. It was often awkwardly silent. I always had the radio on Lite FM. Even the awkwardness inspired . . . poetry.

MAY 23rd

"Owls Can Only See At Night"
An ode to my teacher, Mr. Perkins.

Deep icy eyes
owl-like, mysterious,
hidden behind the glasses.
Fire-glazed, behind the glasses.
I have nothing but mine own eyes.
Naïve, receptive,
Yearning to touch the owl's.
No, I could never let go,
Not after the gifts of sight.
Damn, the love affair of unrequited emotion!
But! He said it was semi-requited!
True. There was . . . one kiss.
But alas, we cannot mix our minds and bodies.
An owl can never make love with the cocoon of a butterfly.

ADULT ME SAYS:

The kiss. It was probably because I'd studied Ovid's *Erotic Poems* in class that day. But for some reason, that afternoon I didn't have to go through my usual song and dance to get him to drive home with me. Instead we lingered in his office, and he actually made eye contact with me, rather than stare nervously at exam papers. Then, in a single motion, he leaped to the door, switched off the lights, turned to me, and murmured, "Are you ready?" Ready? For what? Driving him home? Finding the iambic rhythm in Ovid's poem?

The next thing I knew, I was against the wall, feeling his breath on my face. It was hot, and he smelled fresh but artificial, like Irish Spring soap. I was finally getting what I had wanted for months, but quite franky it felt icky. He was holding me tight, and I was surprised that he was shaking. As we were kissing, I felt the light switch digging into my back. I accidentally rubbed against it, it caught in my bra strap, and the light went on. He instantly pulled away, grabbed his books, and ushered me out. We got in my car as if it had never happened. We didn't say a word to each other all the way home.

MAY 27th

I just saw him in the cafeteria. He pretended he didn't see me. I am bland now, ultimately tasteless. God, I don't know what to do: I crave and crave and crave and crave, yet I can taste nothing left in myself. I sound so ridiculous, I know, but I truly, with every fiber and particle of my being, love him. And what's funny is that if I were *with* him, I wouldn't know what I'd want to do . . . I would love to kiss him again, passionately and kiss in soft pecks on his cheeks. I truly feel connected with him, connected inside, deep within myself. His secretary noticed we were wearing the same color and said, "You two are soul mates." We are in a strange sort of way. I think about him more than I could ever imagine. I adore being with him. It is not that he makes me feel so great about life, but he makes me feel great deep inside and a strange excitement fills my inner void and a thrill rushes out of my eyes.

He brings out in me a Marnie separate from the Marnie I know. He brings out the Inner Marnie, the secret one I can't reach all the time and the one that God would judge. My mother is screaming at me. I have to get ready for dinner. As if anyone can eat at a time like this.

JUNE 3rd

My graduation was yesterday and tomorrow is transition, is change, is growth, is nothing, is UNKNOWN! Everything I say now, I've learned from Mr. Perkins. I desperately need him and all that is left of him is part of me. So I guess I could use me and him in a dialectical process, like:

Marnie = Thesis.

B.P. = Antithesis.

The Unknown = Synthesis.

We meet in the Unknown.

How funny is it that I am comparing my internal, insignificant contradiction with the great Hegelian contradiction that has forever been pondered by philosophers. I feel too attached now, and I wonder if I will be okay when he "cuts the umbilical cord." I love him and I know I am *in love* with him, but I don't know how or why or what I will feel later. He opened my mind, molded me into an amorphous form, and then left me to shape myself . . .

ADULT ME SAYS:

There was, however, one last kiss. It was after a graduation party. We left at the same time. We were alone in the elevator. It was a long ride down. The minute the doors closed, we were in each other's arms. Just as the elevator hit the lobby, we separated. As the doors opened, he gave me a chaste hug good-bye, as if I were any student and he were any teacher. Like an idiot I thanked him for being a good teacher, when what I really wanted to say was, "Darling, when will I see you again?"

After graduation I went to Europe with my best friend, so I knew I'd have time to ponder my deep and enduring connection with BP in the most romantic surroundings, in the most literary way.

AMSTERDAM, JULY 3rd

Here I am in Europe so far away from B.P., but still, he dominates me. I know I am going to get over my idiot-like crush on this man, but it's frustrating that I can't get him out of my head! Shit! I look at men with "the BP look" and hope that they are as intellectually stimulating, but none of them are. Everywhere I turn is another BP Gas Station! I love him with all of my passion in my heart!

LONDON, JULY 15th

Last night in the heat of a silly drunken stupor, I decided to call and hang up on my . . . how should I call him . . . mind-lover. That's a pretty good name,

eh? In any case, I HEARD B.P.'S VOICE! I HEARD IT!!
So HIM, that kind of squeaky mouse-like, yet deeply
masculine voice. Oh. I'm so infatuated, I can not even
describe it.

But in the book I'm reading, *Lady Chatterly's
Lover*, DH Lawrence describes it wonderfully, "Yes,
he was educating her. And he enjoyed it. It gave him
a sense of power. And she was thrilled . . . she was
thrilled to a weird passion . . . and his "educating" her
roused in her a passion of excitement and response
much deeper than any love affair could have done. In
truth, the fact that there could be no love affair, left
her free to thrill to her very marrow . . ." (p93) Does
this not culminate my feelings or what?

AUGUST 3rd

I am home now. I am on my bed writing, but I can't
find a pen, so I'm using my Dad's little golf pencil.
I just called BP and I told him I really don't want to
leave for college. He said: "You can always come back,
but not if you never leave." I absolutely hate writing
in pencils, for if one writes in this *temporary lead*,
he or she will only later look back to one hell of a
smudgy page. I feel sad now, but soon, it will smudge
away.

Every emotion I have can, at one moment, be in
dark magic marker, and at the next, a runny print,
and still at the next, an erasable ink. So, all I know
at this stupid moment is that I'm in a pencil state.
And I can't express the love I feel for BP in a pencil,

because I never want my feelings for him to smudge
away . . .

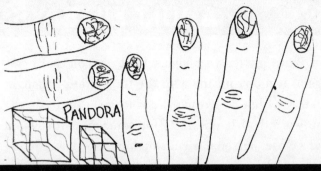

PANDORA

I reluctantly left for college, but after a few months I didn't
long for him anymore. I just wanted him to read all my
papers. When I came back for Thanksgiving, I ran into him
at the supermarket.

NOVEMBER 26th

I saw BP today. It is so bizarre! It utterly fascinates
me that feelings of power and passion and love and
hatred, that vitality and fever, could fade. Really!
Feelings are not here forever, and for the first time
in my life, I am thankful for the CHANGE. To look
into those ice, blue owl-like eyes that once stabbed
excitement into my pitless stomach and now to
feel . . . nothing. No turning and churning in the
lower abdomen—instead, there is a chill-less-ness, an
impenetrable feeling. HE CAN NO LONGER, NOR
WILL HE EVER AGAIN, AFFECT ME, TAMPER

WITH MY LOVE because I don't feel him: Je ne le sais pas. C'est vrai, c'est bien.

ADULT ME SAYS:

It wasn't until my ten-year high school reunion that I saw him again. It didn't fill me with the trepidation I thought it would. All I felt as I reached out to greet him was the genuine warmth that one feels for someone with whom one had a close, personal friendship long ago. After all, my experience with him was pivotal during my formative years, even if it was wholly inappropriate on several levels.

He did not respond in kind. "You've ruined my life," he said. "You could've gotten me fired."

What could I say? Perhaps in my overly florid prose I'd had it right to begin with: "An owl can never make love with the cocoon of a butterfly."

Matt

Kirsten

DUELING DIARIES
Matt Berck and Kirsten Gronfield

↓

Least Likely to . . . File
His Taxes by Himself

↓

Most Likely to . . . Not
Get Kissed Until After
High School

ADULT MATT SAYS:

I was a theater kid in high school with no real romantic history. But, that being said, I was obsessed with the *idea* of being in a relationship. This was further fed by a daily diet of romantic love ballads and evening call-in request radio shows (such as *The Affection Connection*).

Kirsten and I never dated, kissed, or consummated our "relationship" beyond late-night phone calls, written-out song lyrics, and awkward schooltime interactions. (As it happened, I did fall into a relationship with her older sister, Carolyn, as she alludes to below.) And yet, despite all this, we constantly acted as if were in an intense lovers' quarrel. Turns out that, being theater geeks, we didn't so much crave an actual relationship as much as we craved *the drama* of an actual relationship.

ADULT KIRSTEN SAYS:

Yeah. What he said.

KIRSTEN WROTE:
M—
I don't understand. I just don't. I don't . . . I don't . . . understand.

Our relationship is not a song. It's not a soap opera. It's not a painting or a poem. To hell with Romantic Tragedy.

We are real. Granted, so is Phil Collins but he's not singing about *us*. He's not singing to you about me, to me about you. He's singing his songs. He may not even write them. He is getting paid. I'm sorry, I'm not being "artistic" about this.

I'm sorry that I don't understand. I listen to "the" tape and I think we ARE a song, but that's bull. I don't mean to sound angry. I just want to cry.

I wish I had a memory like yours. You always remember word for word what we wrote to each other. I don't even remember which letter you got, or what it said. I did not expect this.

MATT WROTE:
He closed his eyes. The emptiness was back. The pain now came. He absentmindedly grabbed his chest and sighed. He then thought about the sight and how at times they can be the greatest of sensations and the perfect compliment to a favorite emotion. But this was not then and the time was not now.

His room was dark and the music soft. He let his mind go back into the past, for perhaps the last time. He took for granted thinking that the memories were set in stone. As with passing time and pain rubbed the stone down to sand. He looks at the sand, not knowing whether to smile at the warmth he receives from it, or cry at the cold he now must face.

To choose to love someone is a great risk, but to show it, the greatest. He's taken not just the first risk, but both. And he's paid the price.

KIRSTEN WROTE:
I'm basically writing to ask you to send a copy or summary or something about the letter you got from me . . . why it made you cry . . . how you know I've changed . . . Why have I changed? WHY ARE YOU SAYING GOODBYE?!?!?

I expected friendship in this letter. A hand. A smile. You? Damn it, Matt. I don't get it? What did I do wrong? When did I lie?

I'm so upset now . . . I opened the letter at Driver's Ed. All alone outside ripping apart the envelope with anticipation ?????????????????????????? only to find ripped pieces of my heart inside.

Why aren't we friends? Why don't you care about me? WHY do you hate me? WHY ISN'T EVERYTHING GOOD?

Can't I make people happy anymore? What am I good for then? Can't I make everything better? If I can't, why am I alive, Matt? I thought we were friends . . . then you . . . and Carolyn . . . and YOU would finally be perfectly happy. THEN I could be, maybe.

Have I just messed up again?

Matt, why don't you trust me anymore? Why won't you tell me what you're thinking? Why does it hurt so much to think you don't care? Why am I so scared of you? I know. You scare me because you make me feel how you want to, when you want to. And now I am stuck here. Vulnerable. PLEASE WRITE. Or at least send that letter.

MATT WROTE:
In the darkness, a phone rang. He answered it. A lady was on the line.

The voice was slightly melodic but ever so soft. If she were here now though, the voice would give the ears pleasure but his heart would be in her eyes. A sound is easily described in context such as this but a sight of this magnitude and enchantment can only be experienced and not read. As the sparkle is like none other found in the clearest crystal or the most lucid of water.

She had this angel face, but you'd strip her down and there she'd be with this angel face in black panties. I used to want to clench her skin and hold her so tender. She'd feel so small, but I would feel miniscule and yet enormous at the same time. An overpowering wave of emotion of love would fill every void in my body so full—to the point of explosion.

But these are merely traps, he has to tell himself. So he does not let on. He said goodbye, for he had to. Tomorrow is another day and she is a different person.

254

Prose didn't seem to be getting the job done. We had to find a new form to express our anguish. We had built up all this tension between us.

The passion finally culminated in—what else—a collaborative poem. Trading it back and forth, we wrote it during a *Dateline* video presentation in sixth-hour economics. THIS was our sex.

KIRSTEN WROTE:
Please do not frighten me away
now that we shared a wish.
I will not let my passion fray
before we've ever shared a kiss.

MATT WROTE:
I did not mean to scare,
and God knows I don't want to miss
this special bond we've attained,
before we share a kiss

KIRSTEN WROTE:
With chains of hurt you're choking me.
Your antonym lurks near.
But only when the moon is free
can I feel him here.

MATT WROTE:
I realized I was choking you,
but not with warmth or love.
But rather with mixed emotions,
which depended on light above.

KIRSTEN WROTE:
I cannot be the puppeteer
of your days' delight.
Nor can honestly be here
Whenever I am in your sight

MATT WROTE:
With the day brought fright.
My existence became a mirror.
Experiencing not delight,
but reflecting what came near.

KIRSTEN WROTE:
Why couldn't you just let me love?
Let me cherish you?
Instead you cried out wounded blood,
assumed I wasn't true.

MATT WROTE:
I just needed someone to love.
That I showed too well.
But to allow someone to love,
that became my hell.

256

KIRSTEN WROTE:
You placed a knife into my palm,
then stabbed open your soul.
Though framed, you thought me cold and calm
and furrowed in your hole.

MATT WROTE:
All I see is fault
where you showed me care.
Accepting not what you say,
and believing that was fair.

KIRSTEN WROTE:
Reality was suicide.
You won't show your scars.
Instead, in fantasy you hide,
losing what was ours.

MATT WROTE:
This play has been acted out.
Various people in your role.
My character's love in doubt,
for experience stains his soul

ADULT KIRSTEN SAYS:

Matt recently moved to California, near me, and we have remained friends-without-benefits for more than a decade. That's pretty sweet.

ADULT MATT SAYS:

Yeah. What she said.

258

W.H.SMITH

WIDE rules

BACK INTO THE CLOSET

Kevin Wofsy

Most Likely to . . . Play Dress-Up

297x210mm

27380

A4 SIZE • 160 SHEETS • WIDE RULING WITH MARGIN • MADE IN THE UK

When I was seventeen, I graduated from high school, came out of the closet, and spent the summer in San Francisco feeling out and gay and fabulous.

Unfortunately, before that declaration I had signed up for an exchange program beginning that fall at a very *traditional* English boarding school. So when the summer ended, instead of going to college I shipped off to Taunton School in Somerset.

And went *back* into the closet.

With my life suddenly transformed into an endless Jane Austen movie, I was lonely, horny, isolated, frustrated, self-absorbed, and bitter. Even worse, I was still a virgin. My only outlet for all my pent-up gayness—and aggravation at the British way of life—was a series of letters back home to my one gay friend, Chandler, who worked at a pornography shop in the Castro.

10/4/91

Dear Chandler,

I probably shouldn't have gotten drunk in my room again this afternoon, but I couldn't help it. This place is a hell-school. I have come to view it as a zoo; these people are just animals in cages to whom I pleasantly condescend. Superiority complexes are disgusting, it's true, but nobody needs to know that I think everyone here is backward and ignorant. They probably think I'm obnoxious and selfish. The difference is: I'm right and they're wrong.

This morning at breakfast, we were discussing *Truth or Dare* (called *In Bed with Madonna* over here for some reason). The guys at the table could speak of nothing but the kiss between the two guys. All were quick to compete for the title of who had felt the sickest at this sight. Sick with envy, you little fucks!

I'll probably come back in Jan. or Feb. unless I start a beautiful relationship with the blond angelboy who sits across from me in chapel. I think we've been cruising each other. I'll keep you posted.

10/6/91

Dear Chandler,

Angelboy is definitely interested! The cruising in chapel this morning was very choice. I love how his eyes say nothing but: "I want to love you." I think he is my religion right now. Should I cruise more vigorously, lip-licking, winking, etc.? The problem with that is that although it's an unmistakable sign, it can imply that your interest is purely for kinky lustful buttfucking behind the cricket pavilion.

Plus, it could be weird to do it in chapel. As it is now, I don't even know his name. If I don't get to feel his heartbeat against my own before I leave, there is no justice in this world.

10/10/91

Dear Chandler,

I am leading a life, with perfectly reputable details,
but I can't be bothered to tell you about them. My
trip to Bath on Tuesday, my trip to Stratford yesterday.
Read a guidebook if you're interested, but so far
there's no Frommer's Guide to my psyche. Sometimes,
I close my eyes and part my lips and just imagine
being kissed, as if returning to infancy and waiting for
a nipple to suckle.

10/18/91

Listen:

I've fallen in lust with a boy who looks like
Dan Quayle and was the president of the Young
Republicans Club. He's not racist or sexist. I don't
even know what it is about him that makes him a
Republican. Maybe it has to do with money. But really,
he's a perfectly likeable guy, and for Christ's sake,
he's gorgeous and he's gay and he's interested and I'm
desperate.

But why the fuck couldn't he be a liberal? Or a
closeted Republican? Why the fuck does he have to
be the goddamn president of the club?

ADULT ME SAYS:

That guy was another American exchange student in the
next town over, and the reason I thought he was gay and in
love with me was because his leg accidentally brushed up

against mine at a McDonald's. He later slept with several girls and wrote to me about it.

11/8/91
Dear Chandler,
Am I the only guy in the world who's ever had a long-term relationship which never really existed? Just think for a second how frustrated you would feel if you KNEW that the guy you wanted had his eye on you but you couldn't have him. Imagine if all your relationships were stillborn. If your first lover was a miscarriage, and your second had his umbilical cord coiled around his neck.

1/24/92 - 10:51 PM
I'm totally in lust with Angelboy. In fact, I think it is time to ask ourselves just what that boy is. Angelboy is a symbol. He is not reality. He represents the hope that lies within us all of achieving some impossible goal. As Tennessee Williams says, "He is the long-delayed but always expected something that we live for."

2/20/92
Dear Chandler,
I just got back from Scotland and read your letter and now I'm antsy about it. BLOODY HELL! You're fucking this Petie guy and I'm jerking off in the loo of a bloody InterCity 125 train from Edinburgh to Taunton. Do you know how depraved that feels?!!! GIVE ME ANGELBOY OR GIVE ME DEATH!!!

2/24/92

Dear Chandler,

Angelboy talked to me at the disco last night! It
may not seem like big news to you, but it's really
incredible. He said, "Hey Kevin, how're you doing?" I
was ecstatic, needless to say. Well, the thing is, he left
pretty soon after, which was kind of a mixed message.
(Naturally, I fantasize that he went back to his room
and had a good long wank about me, but I digress.)

5/6/92

Dear Chandler,

Sorry I haven't written sooner, but I've been too busy
to do so. Why? I've been spending an incredible
amount of hours with a certain someone since I've
been back from Easter break. Yes, I need not write
the name because you will already know who he is.
Desire incarnate. The definition of cute. Angelboy.
Yesterday, he said to me, "Kev, you're one of my best
mates!"

I know. I've led you on. You're waiting for me to
describe his penis to you, and alas, I cannot. But I'm
now his best friend at this school, and he is happy for
me to spend all of my time with him. I love him. And
even better, he loves me. Granted, he doesn't know it.

Every night when I go over to see him he's
sucking on a popsicle and I absolutely melt.

5/8/92

Dear Chandler,

This is going too far too fast, and I don't know what I want anymore. I just got back from Angelboy's room, and I can't say that the usual desire came flooding into me. Is it possible that he was only a conquest interest, and now that he's virtually putty in my hands, I'm losing interest? It's not fair. Don't make me lose interest in the thing I've been working for months to attain.

He's such a special person, because he manages to be so sweet and optimistic in spite of having no money, no close friends, and no great gift of intellect or talent. But you can't love a human being in the way that you love a puppy dog. God how he needs me! I've read in books about this awful dichotomy that need is at first very attractive and then actually somewhat boring.

I love Angelboy, but I'm afraid my love may be starting to get mixed with pity, and that kills lust. Maybe it's because he had a zit on his cheek.

6/04/92

Dear Chandler,

I really am glad I stuck it out now. This experience has been so incredible. I've really lived the life of an English schoolboy this year. I'm proud of myself for getting through the hard times, and now I feel I deserve a reward. I was thinking about jobs today, what kind I might get when I'm back for the summer.

I want to do something gay. I'd like to work in a bookstore or ice cream parlor or something like that on Castro. That way, I would meet people without having to go to seedy clubs and "flaunt my asshole," as someone I know so politely put it.

I think I need to meet some boys who already know they're gay.

PLAYING HOUSE
Nellie Stevens
Least Likely to . . . Ever Enjoy Camping

At the age of nineteen I left college because I was confused and depressed, and I had no idea what I wanted to do with my life. So of course I did what anyone should do in that situation—got a mall job, got into a serious relationship with a guy named Chad, and moved in with him way too quickly.

This is a glimpse into what happens when adolescents decide to play house—they try to act like grown-ups instead of adults. As you'll see, it's really not much different from the version we played as kids with the exception of rent and furniture.

1995 Journal

Dear Diary,

What can I say about Chad? He's beautiful. Chad, are you too good to be true or are you what I have been suffering all these years to get to? After that night you read me your journal, I have felt just as gaga. You say just what I want to hear. I could love you. I could fall in love with you. FATE. Does it exist? Dude!

It's everything I've ever wanted yet I'm not running around bragging to everyone "I'm falling in love" because I do not need to prove this guy to anybody! I'm so overtired.

271

The Gap kind of sucks but also keeps me very occupied. I feel like a grown woman who works 2 jobs and calls her boyfriend during lunch breaks to tell him how her day has been. Does my family recognize how quickly I switched from your typical L.A. kid who owns a nice car without ever working a day in her life for it to a good hard worker? Sometimes I don't think they do.

Today, I wondered if I am a crazy nympho because I remember the teacher telling us in Female Physiology that if sex interferes with any key part of your life, you are a sex addict and you need help. Well, I was late to my Gap folding class tonight because I was having sex. Now, does this make me an addict or just an idiot?

Chad, I hope we fall in love. I'm getting ga-ga over you.

ADULT ME SAYS:

We began to discuss the possibility of moving in. I was thrilled—so much so that I managed to ignore the warning signs. No matter how glaring.

Dear Diary,
He does not directly try and dominate me but it's things like the physical limitations and what he said tonight. "I hope you'll be clean when we live together." It's hard work. I feel too careful around him these days.

Dear Diary,

I live with him now. Can you fucking believe it? You were there when I met him for Christ's sake. It's been only *two days* but our apartment *already* seems homey! We're both very cozy oriented people so it works . . .

We're gonna get lots of candles and *little things* that cozy people have. It's a little bit domestic but I guess . . . that's OK! He does not act very domestic. We give each other space thus far.

Isn't it strange that *I'm* "the first," my friends have all seemed to be remarking. But it all makes sense. Everything has happened to me early. Except puberty of course.

How weird that I got big breasts at *seventeen*, and I am living with someone at *nineteen*! But knowing me, I could have done it at *fourteen*.

Dear Diary,

Sometimes I wonder if I take advantage of what I have, because it's so comfortable. Things are *supposed* to get dull for a little while when people are so "used to" each other. But as I write this, I realize that there are no "supposed tos" in my life.

He's playing really annoying acid jazz in the other room, and I'm in my Enya sleep mode. But that's OK. Because I'm learning to live "in harmony" with my boyfriend.

Dear Diary,

I feel stifled by anger. Passionate rage towards the one that I truly love. I know it's true because he would not get under my skin like this unless it *was*. I think the only other people who I have ever felt this angry at are my family. And God knows, I love them.

It's like he wants to possess me but also wants to call the shots about space, running free, not feeling too "smothered." I try to kid him and tell him he's the only one but he only seems . . . half interested. He's always down to kiss, but he has his own schedule as to *when* he feels like kissing. Am I walking on eggshells . . . or learning about respecting another's space?

I don't hear "I love you" that much anymore. Which is OK! But it makes me forget *why* we're trying all of this in the first place.

It's pretty pathetic that in some ways, I *like* when I get angry with him and he is in the wrong, because this means that he can be vulnerable and loving . . . which he is! Maybe he feels so comfortable at this point that he need not show it anymore.

We must keep the relationship fresh.

I am sick of him.

ADULT ME SAYS:

After just six months of this domestic bliss (including three breakups and reconciliations in the process) Chad and I split up permanently. I moved back home with my parents and realized that growing into an adult would be a much slower process than I thought. And to be honest, this was a huge relief.

I had no regrets. Trying on the happy housewife persona taught me some important lessons and had no long-term negative effects. Except, of course, my hatred of acid jazz.

WHAT THE HELL HAPPENED?

Jennifer Anthony divides her time between educational research and writing for a not-for-profit think tank, international travel, volunteering for Big Brothers Big Sisters, and trying out crazy things like skydiving and trapeze school. She has made great strides since her prepubescent dreams of becoming a professional ice cream scooper.

Kate Augustine lives in Chicago, where she works (fittingly) as a headhunter, competes regularly in triathlons and half marathons, and uses her liver as a petri dish. She has successfully escaped her life as a likely combination of teacher/volleyball coach/volunteer firewoman in Ohio.

Sherry Richert Belul is a writer and editor in San Francisco. She owns a one-of-a-kind tribute-book business, ninety-three hats, and five boxes of journals. Sherry has spent the past twenty-five years of her life trying to shake the goody-goody cheerleader image she had in high school.

Matt Berck is an actor in Los Angeles. The only thing he struggles with is mornings.

Liz Black is sometimes a music reviewer, occasionally a copywriter, and always a Red Sox fan. She has written and performed in several sketch shows in New York City over the past five years.

Lucinda Blackwood has been a travel agent, interior designer, actress, aide to a governor, campaign manager, and aide to a big-city mayor. Although she got engaged for the first time at sixteen, it was years before she actually took the plunge. She and her husband and partner of fifteen years celebrated their *first* anniversary in August 2007. She's the proud mother of June, a gifted Jack Russell terrier. She would like to take this opportunity to publicly apologize to her parents, Dick and Billy Jo, for all the sleepless nights and any embarrassment her romantic escapades may have caused.

Lorelei Hill Butters lives in Southern California with her dreamy husband, Darrin, and their two outstanding cats.

Jane Cantillon is a veteran television producer and filmmaker who has received critical acclaim for her documentary *The Other Side: A Queer History.* She happily lives in Hollywood with her husband and teenage daughter.

Erin Carter lives in Edmonton, Alberta, where she is a college-dropout waitress who wishes she were a writer. Growing up in the small tourist town of Sylvan Lake, Alberta, she wasn't the most talkative soul, and maybe she still is not. She used her journals in junior high and high school to say the things she was too timid to talk about.

Laura Chapman works as a paralegal in her favorite city, Chicago. Although at her best while obsessing over something or someone, she's happy to report that she's been "Whitey-free" for more than thirty-five years and has made a solemn vow never to tell anyone else to take a piece of her heart.

Lacy Coil gave up her dreams of working on a sheep farm and guiding hitchhiking tours and is now an actor who shows up on TV, in the occasional movie, and in a lot of plays. She does a lot of Shakespeare but is pretty much over the whole Morrissey thing.

Karen Corday is a librarian. She is still an obsessive diary keeper, twenty years later. She lives in Somerville, Massachusetts, with her husband, who is not named Michael.

Shay DeGrandis serves as the director of academic programs for the School of the Art Institute of Chicago. She resides in Chicago, where she runs the lives of many people. She has become fairly desirable and actually smiles quite often.

GJ Echternkamp is a filmmaker and performer. His documentary *Frank & Cindy* is featured on season one of Showtime's *This American Life* TV series, and his work can be viewed at bionicfilms.com.

Kirsten Gronfield is an actor and writer in Los Angeles and still struggles with poetry.

Leonard Hyman is a documentary filmmaker and stand-up comedian, but mostly an office temp, working in Los Angeles, California.

Boni Joi received her MFA in creative writing from Columbia University. Her poems have appeared in *Arabella, Long Shot, Big Hammer, Mind Gorilla,* and *The Brooklyn Rail.* She performs at numerous venues in New York and elsewhere.

Justin Jorgensen is the author of *Obscene Interiors: Hardcore Amateur Décor.* After a childhood in Fargo, North Dakota, he now lives in Los Angeles, where he designs theme parks and tells dirty stories over fine wines. Visit him online at justinspace.com to see what he's up to.

Colleen Kane has been a writer and editor for *BUST* and *Playgirl* magazines, and has also contributed to *Spin, Radar,* and *Anthem.* She finally swore off dating musicians but lives with her long-haired boyfriend and their ludicrously awesome music collection. She's currently writing her first book when not procrastinating with her blog, cokanesbloggery.blogspot.com.

Angie Lawson is in med school, likely studying even as you read this. She still has a life-size cardboard Spock, which she keeps in her basement in Columbus, Ohio, and moves around periodically to freak out her roommate.

Scott Lifton currently resides in San Francisco, where he enjoys digging through people's pasts and psyches while producing *Mortified*'s San Francisco chapter. He is healthy, not in prison, and still maintains a poor bowling average.

Jami Mandl is an activity director with a specialty in Alzheimer's disease. She has managed to parlay her love of demented people and a desire to do something useful into a fairly successful career.

Laurent Martini is the best antiques dealer/lead singer of Live Evil named Laurent Martini in San Francisco. Thanks to *Mortified*, they finally exist. Rock out with them online at liveevilrocks.com.

MCC is an actor, writer, and comedian. You probably don't know him . . . but if you've seen him before, it most likely was in your wildest dreams.

Leslie McLean lives in Oakland, California, where she works as a reading teacher at an inner-city school. She is both disturbed and delighted that her material still rings true.

R.P. has grown up from her angry emo roots and is now an elementary school teacher. She still has to make threats from time to time, but mostly they are threats of detention, accompanied by that evil eye that all teachers have. She is still with Bill.

Brian Polak decided to once again pick up his pen, despite several years of writing horrible poems as a teen, and start writing plays as an adult. He is now a playwright living in Los Angeles with his wife and writing partner, Jami Brandli, and their many pets. He never ended up dating Jocelyn.

Marnie Pomerantz lives with her three dogs—Caviar, Jasmine, and Biffer—and a great guy named Neil in LA. She still keeps a journal.

Carrie Seim has written for National Geographic Television, *Newsday*, the *Chicago Reporter*, and Channel One and has also had a recurring role on E! network's *Seven Deadly Hollywood Sins*. An alum of the Groundlings Sunday Company, she recently performed her original sketch comedy show *Midwestern Wisdom* at the Comedy Central Stage in Los Angeles. Carrie has yet to outgrow her seventh-grade love of emotionally unavailable boys.

Johanna Stein is a writer and performer hailing from the cultural mecca of Winnipeg, Manitoba. She has acted in some cool movies (*Mulholland Drive*) and some not-so-cool ones (*Appendix A*). She has performed comedy on some cool TV shows (Oxygen's *Ripe Tomatoes*, *The Late Late Show with Craig Kilborn*) and has even directed some of them (Comedy Central's *We're with the Band*). Johanna's parents are particularly proud of the award-winning writing she's done in the field of children's animation.

Nellie Stevens is a writer who in her spare time enjoys dachshunds, pomegranates, and expensive bath products. She currently resides in Los Angeles with her fiancé, who, thankfully, is not one of the guys from her diary entries.

Sean Sweeney is a director and actor, originally from Detroit, now living in Los Angeles. He has appeared in numerous films and television shows as well as more than one hundred commercials around the world.

Maurissa Tancharoen, a recovered child pop star (of the girl group Pretty in Pink), now writes and produces for film and television. She still sings on other people's albums but mostly executive-produces stuff and makes tons of cash. She can be seen running the streets of Los Angeles with her fiancé, Jed.

Kevin Wofsy writes junk e-mail for a technology company in San Francisco. When he isn't urging people to "CLICK HERE AND SAVE!" he writes humiliating, thinly veiled stories about his past. He hopes to have his first novel on the shelves soon. See what he's up to at kevinwofsy.com.

Charles Young was born and raised in Clinton, Massachusetts. He attended Emerson College in Boston and was a touring musician for five years. He is now a proud father and husband living in his hometown.

ABOUT MORTIFIED

Ripped from the pages of real life, *Mortified* celebrates ordinary people and the extraordinary things they created as kids.

A comic excavation of awkward adolescent artifacts—letters, lyrics, poetry, plays, schoolwork, journals, home movies, fiction, artwork—the project encourages people to share their forgotten juvenilia with the modern world. From deluded grade-school love letters to jaded high-school journals, Mortified sifts through our cultural shoebox to unearth our hidden histories. Once selected, each piece is then presented around a unique autobiographical narrative that emerges from its content. In keeping with the spirit of authenticity, no language is ever added or altered to the source material. There are amazing tales buried in the pages of everyone's life. It's our mission to help find them.

Anchored by acclaimed stage shows, popular books, online shorts, and more, *Mortified* is the largest and longest-running organization of its kind. The national grassroots comedy collective is overseen by David Nadelberg and Neil Katcher and supported by a vast network of talented freaks, geeks, and friends across the planet.

For more information on how you can help share the shame, visit getmortified.com.